Let's have a meeting

Let's have a meeting

A comprehensive guide to making your meetings work

Leslie Rae

McGRAW-HILL BOOK COMPANY

London · New York · St Louis · San Francisco · Auckland
Bogotá · Caracas · Lisbon · Madrid · Mexico
Milan · Montreal · New Delhi · Panama · Paris · San Juan
São Paulo · Singapore · Sydney · Tokyo · Toronto

Published by
McGRAW-HILL Book Company Europe
Shoppenhangers Road, Maidenhead, Berkshire SL6 2QL, England
Telephone 0628 23432
Fax 0628 770224

British Library Cataloguing in Publication Data
Rae, Leslie
  Let's Have a Meeting: Comprehensive Guide
  to Making Your Meetings Work
  I. Title
  658.456

ISBN 0-07-707628-1

Library of Congress Cataloging-in-Publication Data
Rae, Leslie.
    Let's have a meeting : a comprehensive guide to making your
  meetings work/Leslie Rae.
      p.   cm.
    Includes bibliographical references and index.
    ISBN 0-07-707628-1
    1. Meetings—Handbooks, manuals, etc.   I. Title.
HF5734.5R33   1994
658.4'56—dc20
                                                            93-43264
                                                              CIP

1234 CUP 97654

Typeset by Book Ens Limited, Baldock, Herts
Printed and bound in Great Britain at the University Press, Cambridge.

Contents

Preface   **ix**

Part One   **1**
1   Introduction   **3**
    Common criticisms   3
    The criticisms answered   4
    The advantages of holding meetings   4
    The golden rules   5
    Aims and objectives   6
    Questions to ask   6
    What are the alternatives?   7

2   Preparing for the meeting—people   **15**
    What is the purpose of the meeting?   15
    What types of meeting are there?   16
    The three-stage meeting process   18
    Preparation involving people   19
    Timing factors   22

3   Preparing for the meeting—the environment   **25**
    Location of the meeting   25
    Seating   26
    Positioning members   31
    Meeting costs   32

4   Planning the meeting   **34**
    Objectives and agenda   34
    Agenda guidelines   37
    Agenda format   37
    The effective agenda   40
    An alternative agenda   44

5   **Final arrangements**   **48**
     Agenda analysis   48
     Final pre-meeting tasks   51

6   **Chairperson behaviour**   **57**
     Chairperson styles   57
     Meeting variations   57
     Decision-making processes   60
     Leadership styles   61
     Behaviour awareness   64
     Behaviour categorization   65
     Behaviour analysis applied to meetings   66
     The effective chairperson   68

7   **Structuring the meeting**   **71**
     The start of the meeting   71
     The main part of the meeting   72
     The end of the meeting   81
     Summary   81

8   **After the meeting**   **83**
     Post-meeting recording   83
     The action note   83
     Minutes   86

9   **Controlling the members**   **94**
     Member problem types   94
     Group behaviour   103

10   **Discussion leading**   **106**
     The role of the discussion leader   106
     Preparation   106
     Objectives   107
     The topic   107
     Analysing a topic   108
     During the discussion   109
     Starting the discussion   110
     Maintaining the discussion   111
     Questioning   112
     Ending the discussion   112

11   Team briefing and brainstorming meetings   **114**
Team briefing   114
The structure of team briefing   115
Preparation for team briefing   120
Brainstorming meetings   120
The form of a brainstorming meeting   123
The organization of brainstorming meetings   124
Decision making following brainstorming   125
The decision process   126

12   Large and formal meetings   **127**
Large meetings   127
The meeting secretary   128
The structure of the large, formal meeting   130
Law and meetings   136

Part Two   **139**
13   Being a member   **141**
Behaviour of members   141
Membership effectiveness   144
At the meeting   147
Game playing   150
The dirty tricks department   152
Planned aggression   152
Delaying tactics   153
Let's put it in writing   154
Meetings in other countries   155

14   Aids to contributions   **157**
Should presentational aids be used?   157
Presentational aids made available   158
Visual aid common features   159
Presentational aids   164
Other aids to presentations   173

15   Using charts and diagrams   **175**
Tabulated data   175
Chart forms   177
Illustrations   188

16 Conclusion **190**
A summary of effective meeting requirements 190

References and recommended reading **192**

Index **193**

Preface

In industry, commerce, voluntary and social organizations a common cry is 'Oh no, not another meeting—surely there must be a better way'. In some cases there are better ways, often not even considered because the tradition of holding a meeting is so ingrained. But in many more cases a meeting is the more appropriate, economic and effective approach. What causes most people to make the opening remark is because they have suffered meetings which have been run badly, for the wrong reasons and with ineffective results. Convert these events into enjoyable and productive events and the suggestion 'Let's have a meeting' will not be greeted with derision.

The purpose of this book is to try to suggest ways in which meetings of almost every variety can be moved into the latter category, or if a new series is starting, to ensure that this is the atmosphere from the start. It will not be easy for managers and others who take on chairpersons' roles to practise these effective techniques if for years they have developed a pattern which has been maintained only because of a captive audience.

The book is aimed at managers (of all levels), supervisors, team leaders, and anybody else who on occasions has to arrange and hold a meeting. Also included is a chapter especially directed at members of meetings to help them to improve their own performance and the effectiveness of the meeting at the same time.

I should like to thank all the people, chairpersons and members with whom I have worked in meetings for reinforcing my views on what makes an effective meeting. Many managers and supervisors have passed through training events which I have held to try to assist any improvements, and I have even been invited to real meetings by some of my trainees to show me how they had taken my training to heart and practice. I thank these people for the many lessons they taught me. Some research has been done into meeting effectiveness and this is included with due reference to the sources.

My intention in writing was to produce a guidebook which would contain as many different approaches and techniques as possible relating to meetings. From this information anyone concerned with managing meetings could extract methods, techniques and approaches with which they were not familiar and try them out in their real meetings. So the book is basically a self-development guide, but is also a reference book for individual aspects of meetings to which reference can be made if help is wanted on specific aspects. Finally, many trainers are required to mount managing meeting training events: I hope they too will find the book useful by extracting material for tutorial sessions and as feedback checks when they include meeting activities.

The book is divided into two parts: Part One contains my guidelines and tips for chairpersons of meetings; Part Two reverses the approach and looks at meetings more from the members' point of view, although chairpersons will also benefit. I should like to thank my wife, Susan, and my two boys, Alex and Oliver, for once again putting up with my frequent visits to my computer denying them my time. Thanks must also go to Julia Riddlesdell and Lavinia Porter of McGraw-Hill for their help in bringing the manuscript to publication.

Because of sex discrimination attitudes, the traditional 'chairman' title has fallen into disuse, but no satisfactory replacement has been found. Variations include 'chair' and 'chairperson' in addition to 'chairman' when a man is involved and 'Madame Chairman' if a woman is involved—although the latter is approaching the boundary of sex rejection. My personal choice is 'chairperson' rather than an inorganic reference to a 'chair'; but that is a matter of preference, and this is the term used throughout, with one exception when I refer to research which was directed at the time at 'chairmen'.

Leslie Rae

PART ONE

PART ONE

Chapter 1

Introduction

One of the most common statements in commerce and industry, made when someone raises a problem or interesting aspect, is 'Let's have a meeting about it'. This suggestion is met with a variety of responses, spoken or not, the response depending on the individual's experiences with meetings. The responses can include

- 'Oh no. Not another *** meeting!'
- 'Do I have to come?'
- 'I might have known this would happen!'
- 'We always have to have a meeting!'
- 'I can't afford the time.'
- 'The boss will decide anyway!'

Common criticisms

Members who have to attend meetings criticize them for the following reasons:

- 'Too frequent—can't get on with my work.'
- 'Too long—some people seem to think that if a meeting doesn't last a day it isn't a good meeting.'
- 'They are just talking shops—people talking too much and for too long.'
- 'Nothing ever seems to get done.'
- 'Even if we decide anything, frequently nothing happens after the meeting.'
- 'The meeting is just called so the boss can tell us what he or she has decided before we even meet.'
- 'The noisy ones always seem to get their own way.'
- 'So that everybody can be satisfied, the final decision is so watered down that it is useless.'
- 'Everybody is just playing games.'

- 'Think of how much this waste of time is costing.'
- 'Did we really need to have a meeting for this?'

The criticisms answered

Not every meeting is ineffective or unsuccessful and unenjoyable, but many are. What are the differences? Some of the answers to these questions are contained in the comments of people who have attended 'good' meetings. These include:

- 'I knew exactly what the meeting was about and why I was there.'
- 'We all knew what the meeting had been called for and what result was intended.'
- 'Everybody had a chance to have a say, but nobody was allowed to hog the discussion.'
- 'Everybody seemed to want to help everybody else and to get the best result.'
- 'I learned a lot because I could listen rather than have to force my way in.'
- 'The chairperson certainly knew how to keep the meeting in order without bullying.'
- 'When I put forward an idea, everybody seemed to listen then looked for everything good in it.'
- 'The meeting was essential and we took the minimum amount of time necessary to resolve the situation.'

However, meetings of this effective nature just do not happen without a catalyst—the effective chairperson. The purpose of this book is to give you as many guidelines as possible to help you become that elusive person.

The advantages of holding meetings

With all the complications and potential problems which help to reduce the effectiveness of meetings, why have meetings at all? If performed effectively, some of the advantages of meetings are as follows:

- They save time by bringing a number of people together to discuss and decide something, rather than trying to deal with it in another way, e.g. in writing or dealing with people one at a time.

- They give an opportunity for various views to be expressed, listened to, discussed and decided upon.
- They encourage good communication, coordination, improved relationships and co-working.
- They ensure that everyone involved in a subject has an opportunity to make his or her views known and to hear the views of others.
- They enable the extent of support for proposals or ideas to be assessed.
- They encourage speakers to clarify and/or justify their views when expressed before others, thus making them consider their views more carefully and construct clear presentations.
- They enable the pooling of knowledge, skills and resources of people who do not normally work together.
- They can ensure the spreading of tasks among a number of people.
- They stimulate the thought processes of participants through the example of others.
- They build working relationships among people from different parts of the company or different organizations.
- They help to establish a uniformity or commonality of attitude and action within a group, department or company or group of organizations.
- They help to increase the self-confidence and creativity of individuals either in a leader (chairperson) role or as a member, particularly in a group or team situation. Some individuals may not bring forward ideas when they are working alone, but in the atmosphere of meeting interaction they are encouraged to express themselves or be creative, particularly when they hear others speak out with less valuable contributions.

The golden rules

Simplified as far as possible, the golden rules for holding effective meetings are the following:

- Ensure that the meeting is set up properly and nothing is left to chance.
- The chairperson must be effective, efficient and follow the appropriate role for the situation.
- The members should have the opportunity to contribute fully in an interactive atmosphere of support.

- Unless there are any specific reasons to the contrary, the meeting participants should enjoy the meeting.

Aims and objectives

If you are caught up in the essential business need of holding meetings, your first action must be to question the 'essential' nature of these events:

- Can the number of meetings you are required to hold be reduced in number?
- Can the number of people attending the meetings be reduced?
- Can the length of time used by the meeting be reduced?

Obviously it will not always be possible to satisfy these objectives—the number of meetings may already be the minimum number necessary to achieve the specific aims; all the people who attend are essential to the effectiveness of the meeting; a particular length of time is required to achieve a specific objective. But there are few occasions when effectiveness cannot be improved by modification of existing practices.

Questions to ask

You have been given the task of finding the solution to a complex problem, requiring the skill input of a number of people; you need to have as many opinions as possible on a subject so that a decision can be made or a recommendation passed to a higher authority; you have or have been given information which must be passed to the workforce. The traditional answer to these situations is 'Let's have a meeting'. Is this the most effective way of achieving the particular objective?

Here are the basic questions which must be posed when you are placed in this position (or decide that doubts arise about holding a meeting):

1 What is the purpose of meeting? What are the objectives?
2 Do we need to have a meeting to achieve these objectives?
3 What types of meeting are there?
4 What other methods could be used?
5 Of these options, including a meeting, which one is likely to be the most effective?
6 If a meeting appears to be the most effective, why?

7 When should the meeting be held? Day, time?

8 Where should the meeting be held? Workplace, my office, boardroom, somebody else's office, etc.?

9 What form should the meeting take?

10 How long could it last to be cost-effective?

11 Who should attend? Why?

12 How should the meeting progress?

13 (And once again) Should we have a meeting at all?

The guidelines in this book should enable you to satisfy your objectives if you are to be the chairperson of a meeting or set of meetings. But first, let us look at the alternatives.

What are the alternatives?

Alternatives to group meetings can include:

- A face-to-face, one-to-one meeting
- A telephone call to another person
- A telephone or video conference call
- A memorandum
- A bulletin posting or newsletter (particularly when it is only necessary to impart information)
- A written questionnaire or sought solution
- A Delphic type of questionnaire approach
- The grapevine
- No action

Face-to-face, one-to-one meeting

This is perhaps the most common occasion on which we hold meetings, often the result of a pre-arrangement, but also the very common informal, quickly arranged meeting as the result of a chance encounter in the corridor. However, if it seems likely that such a meeting is possible, preparation for it must be attempted to the maximum extent possible. Most of the planning and presentation aspects we shall be considering later will be relevant to this face-to-face encounter. Both parties must be aware of the purpose of the meeting—decision, discussion, exchange of views, etc. and both must be well prepared with all the data about the topic at their disposal.

Advantages
In an effective interaction these can include:

- A considerable saving of time as only two people are involved and extraneous arguments do not get in the way.
- Time and timing arrangements are simpler as only two people have to be satisfied.
- No special location, etc., arrangements need to be made.
- An informal atmosphere can be generated readily.
- Verbal and non-verbal interactions are clear. If they are not, clarification can be obtained easily and without any possible loss of face on the part of the questioner, as there are no others present to observe his or her non-understanding.
- Usually two views only are to be presented and eventual agreement reached on one—the more people present, the more likely there are to be more views.
- Complete and undivided attention (ignoring external distractions), one for the other, ensuring real listening and understanding.

Possible disadvantages
Disadvantages might include:

- Embedded conflict of views from the start of the interaction.
- Views and ideas are limited to those held by two people only.
- Others are excluded from what might seem to be a closed pairing.
- The issue is too complicated for the expertise of the two participants.
- Opposing values and value judgements may get in the way of realistic decision making.
- Other people may need to have an input into the discussion and decisions.

So, superficially, meetings involving two people only can appear to be an ideal, whereas this may not always be so in practice.

Alternative face-to-face approaches
The immediate interpretation of this type of meeting is of two people in the same location, but variations of this are possible.

The people concerned might be in widely separate locations, so if you want to hold a meeting they may have to travel some distance to your location or you may have to travel to their unit to meet. This presents little problem if only one meeting is involved, or only one person is involved. But if a number of people are involved and a central group meeting is not feasible, a series of one-to-one meetings can satisfy the requirement.

In addition to the disadvantages described above, there are also the following considerations:

- The extra expenditure of time and money with several people and locations.
- The possible omission or addition of discussion items at the various meetings.
- The absence of any opportunity for an immediate exchange of views, disagreement and support between all the people involved.

If such a course of action is impossible to avoid, and there will be occasions when it is the appropriate action to take, the initiator should:

- Calculate the most economical travel pattern, taking into account the availability of each person.
- Confirm immediately before travelling that no changes in arrangements have had to be made.
- Produce an agenda of items to discuss with detailed insets of specific aspects of each item. This agenda or 'shopping list' should be used actively during each individual discussion to ensure uniformity.
- Ensure that all the participants are aware of the views of the others before any final decision is made. This will give them the opportunity—in writing, telephone or personal visit—to present their views on the ideas of others.

Telephone conversations
The telephone as an alternative to a group meeting has many similarities to the one-to-one, face-to-face meeting or series of meetings, but without the advantage of visual contact.

In circumstances when face-to-face meetings of any nature are impossible—for example when considerable distances separate the parties—this may be the best alternative. However, the telephone depersonalizes communication and many people are not at ease discussing issues, particularly complex or emotive ones, over the phone. The principal loss is the visual image. We are used to and prefer to see the person to whom we are talking, and with the other person before you any non-verbal signals which either reinforce or contradict the verbal message might be visible.

Otherwise the telephone approach is similar to the face-to-face visit. The principal guidance is that you should always have an 'agenda' of some nature which you can mark off as you complete discussion on each item. A common feature of telephone contact is the realization, immediately after the line has been cut, that something has been omitted.

Unless you particularly want to place the other at a disadvantage by placing the phone call and entering cold into the 'meeting', it is helpful to give some warning of the phone discussion perhaps by a short 'preface' call. This gives the other person the same opportunity you have had to do some research, obtain some data, consider any position held and be in a position to respond.

It is certainly advisable, however, at the end of the call to ensure that a clear, complete summary is made and when the call is completed to send this summary of agreements to the other party.

Conference calls
In this alternative a group of colleagues based in, say, London meet in a room there and contact a similar group congregated in another location. The two locations are connected by a telephone link and at each location there are loudspeakers or headphones and a microphone. The members contribute to the discussion *almost* as if they were meeting in one room.

The 'almost' is because this method has the problem that the separated groups cannot see each other and each contributor may have to identify himself or herself when speaking. Interruptions will have to be avoided, although some systems ensure that this cannot happen. Fax machines have eased one of the earlier difficulties, that of the problem of immediate access to papers which are produced.

It is now possible, although at very high cost, to amalgamate the telephone conference call with a closed circuit television link. This obviously solves some of the problems of the non-visual aspects of the telephone conference and with continual improvement in television techniques and equipment, with a consequent reduction in cost, this approach may be much more widely used in the future for national and international meetings.

Memoranda
A memorandum is useful when the principal or sole reason for communication is to give information or issue instructions which do not require discussion. To avoid misinterpretation or misunderstanding, the written words of the memorandum must be clear, understandable and unambiguous. This is the principal possible disadvantage of the memo—

the written word can so easily be misinterpreted or misunderstood even when the writer feels that the meaning is clear.

Words such as 'quite', 'rather', 'average' must not be used, and there is every danger that many readers will place their own interpretations on descriptions. When this is the only opportunity of giving the information, if it is misunderstood, there may be no way that problems ensuing from the misunderstanding can be rectified easily.

The sending of a memorandum giving information implies that the sender is confident that all the recipients will *see* the memo and *read* it. Unfortunately, there is no guarantee that either of these assumptions will be satisfied.

Newsletter
The newsletter can take the place of memoranda in a large organization when information has to be disseminated to a large group. Problems arise when newsletters are either very frequent occurrences or are rare—each has its problem. Too frequent receipt produces the risk that they will not be read; rarity might mean that information contained may be out of date.

Other problems include:

- There is no guarantee that everybody will receive a copy.
- There is no guarantee that all recipients will read it.
- Without some form of back-up, misinterpretations or non-understandings can occur.

Bulletin board
In theory, posting an item of information on the bulletin board should ensure that everybody in the organization will have the opportunity of seeing and reading it. However, the approach is open to the following disadvantages:

- Misunderstanding or non-understanding.
- Misinterpretation.
- No opportunity to resolve queries.
- The board may not be looked at.
- Board hygiene is ignored.

However, if some attempts are made to provide information back-up to notices posted and well-maintained boards are located conveniently, this medium can be very effective in communicating information to the total workforce.

Written questionnaires

This can be a useful approach when the people from whom a view is required are relatively limited in number and are located so widely that a meeting would be impossible or uneconomic, and telephone contact might not produce the definitive information required.

Before commencing the process, the seeker of the information must decide:

- What is the specific information required?
- What is the minimum number of views required?
- Who are the people who could/should give these views?
- What question format will ensure that the questions are clear and unambiguous and incapable of misinterpretation?

The comments made about memoranda apply equally here, but there is one important addition—*an arrangement must be included for the date of the return of the questionnaire.*

Question format will be determined by the type of information required and will include either open or closed questions. If wide views on a non-specific item are required, the question can be open: 'What are your views on the introduction of an appraisal scheme?' If, for example, the subject of the introduction of the scheme has already been discussed and it is now time for final decisions, the question might be expressed in a closed manner: 'Do you agree or disagree with the introduction of the appraisal system?' This latter type of question can provide the opportunity for the recipients to write their answers, or a YES/NO option might be given, or there may even be the opportunity for multiple choices to be offered.

In most cases the answers to questionnaires need to be collated and analysed. If there are many responses, and these are complex, non-uniform and open, the more difficult the analysis becomes. This commends the use of closed question types of questionnaires, but these restrict the wider expression of views. Both approaches may require further contact to share the views expressed and determine attitudes to various views offered.

The Delphi technique

This is a questioning approach to a number of people from whom views are required so that a decision might be made, using the various views of the participants. It can be viewed as an extension beyond the previous straightforward questioning technique.

The relevant questionnaires are sent to a number of people with an interest and experience in the subject on which a decision has to be made. When the responses are received they are analysed and demonstrated statistically, usually showing the frequency of similar views. The distribution analysis is then circulated among the ones who answered the original questionnaire in addition to a summary of all the views. They are then asked, particularly those who responded with views outside the middle range, whether they wish to reconsider their answers. The responses to this approach usually show a swing towards the middle range: if not, then there must be a very serious examination of the extreme views. The modified responses are again analysed according to the distribution frequency, and the questionnaire completers are given a further opportunity to revise their views. The question is usually by then in a state for a decision to be made, everybody having had the opportunity to give the matter their fullest consideration and also the chance for them to change their minds having seen other arguments.

The grapevine

The grapevine is usually considered to be the way a rumour is spread among the workforce of an organization, the details of the rumour often being inaccurate and based on something half-overheard. Although many people realize that a grapevine message is often only a rumour, a half-truth or perhaps completely inaccurate, it usually permeates to all the workforce and is accepted by all who hear it.

The method is obviously not to be recommended as a prime approach. But it exists and it is possible on occasions to make use of it to disseminate official and accurate information throughout the organization, speedily and completely by setting off the 'rumour' at the management level, rather than always being on the receiving end of the rumouring. It must, of course, be accepted that the message may become contaminated in its progress. But there will be occasions when absolute accuracy is not all important.

But use this method with care and with awareness of all the problems attached.

No action

Having considered all the possible alternatives to holding a meeting, the conclusion is reached that the information or action is not worth the expenditure of everybody's time, or perhaps the time is not yet ripe for the information to be revealed/discussed. The option in this situation is to take no action at all.

Meetings, if they are to be the important aspect of an organization's operation—as they should be—should not be treated or held lightly, but should be held only when they are the most appropriate action to take and alternatives have been considered. People will then start to appreciate their value and the meetings will stop being '**** meetings'!

Chapter 2

Preparing for the meeting— people

By this stage you have decided that in order to satisfy your objectives, a meeting is the method by which they will be most effectively achieved. Before you can get down to aspects of the meeting itself there are a number of subjects that must be decided if the meeting has any chance of being successful.

What is the purpose of the meeting?

Once you have decided to hold a meeting, you must have a very clear idea of what is to be achieved. The first stage is to define the objectives as clearly and as specifically as possible. This may be simply a question of clear definition, but it might also be one of redefinition.

Defining meeting objectives
The objectives for a meeting can be to decide the following:

- In clear precise, unambiguous terms, what are we setting out to achieve?
- In what period of time do we want/need/have to achieve it?
- To what levels do we need to achieve? Understanding, problem solving, decision making, agreeing, producing (e.g. a report), etc?

Types of objectives
The objectives for a meeting can be:

- Singular and discrete
- Multi-aspected on a singular theme
- Multi-aspected on a range of subjects

A typical example of a singular objective meeting might be a decision about whether or not redundancies should be made. This could be developed into a multi-aspected objective:

1 To decide whether the financial situation would be best resolved by spreading the company's investments.
2 If an investment policy is agreed, to decide how many and which investments; how much to invest and any other criteria.
3 To decide when the most favourable time will occur to make the investments.

Very commonly, your meeting will be multi-aspected over a range of different subjects. The objectives for this type of meeting might appear as:

1 To agree the month's accounts against the budget proposals.
2 To decide on the recruitment policy for temporary staff.
3 To discuss and agree the month's production figures and decide on any necessary action.
4 To discuss and decide whether the financial situation would be best resolved by spreading the company's investments, and if so to decide how many investments, how much and any other criteria.

Definition of the objectives in the clearest terms will help to produce a meeting agenda that is:

- realistic in terms of what can be done by the membership,
- realistic in terms of what can be done in the time allocated to the meeting,
- not so varied that a large number of people will need to attend the meeting for parts only,
- sufficiently clear and precise for the membership.

What types of meeting are there?

The objectives determined for the meeting will decide the nature of the meeting, and although there are many similarities, you will be able to decide from your objective the particular type of meeting you need.

The information-giving meeting

In practice this is a misnomer, if we are to consider effective meetings. Any meeting which consists of the manager/leader/chairperson simply giving out information hardly qualifies for the title 'meeting'. But an effective meeting of this nature will confirm whether the information has been heard, understood and accepted or rejected. Consequently after the information giving there must be information seeking to test whatever level of receiving is needed, i.e. simply hearing, ensuring understanding, and so on.

The information-seeking meeting

This is the converse of the type of meeting described above, with the intention of determining the views and opinions of a group of people about a subject which has probably been previously communicated in writing. Initially there is a small element of information giving during which the chairperson may summarize the information to ensure everyone is aware of the subject. The effective chairperson then keeps quiet, having posed the required question. Apart from this, the chairperson's role is to ensure that all members of the meeting who wish to contribute are given the opportunity to do so, points of difficulty are answered and the chairperson fully understands the responses he or she is given.

The consultative or general meeting

This type of meeting combines both the types described above. It commonly takes the form of a verbal presentation by the chairperson or other member of a proposal or suggestion put forward for consideration by the meeting membership. The basic form of this meeting stops at this considerative level and, following a discussion in which all views are expressed, a general consensus of agreement or disagreement is reached. The chairperson then, being aware of the views of the meeting members, takes away these views for consideration and perhaps decision.

The problem-solving and decision-making meeting

This is very similar to the consultative meeting with the major difference being that when the proposal has been aired and views collected, the meeting has the authority and responsibility to make a decision. The objectives of a meeting of this nature can be singular, multi-aspected with one topic or multi-aspected with a number of topics, the latter probably being the most common type.

The brainstorming meeting

Before, during or after a decision-making meeting, a brainstorming meeting might be held. The purpose of this meeting is to generate as many ideas, views or solutions to a problem as possible. The results of this meeting are then relayed either to a singular decision maker or to a decision-making meeting group for selection of the preferred or most effective solution.

The team briefing meeting

This is a particular type of meeting which can combine the information-giving, information-seeking and general discussion forms. Although as a meeting it has specific task objectives, because it is part of the team process, there are also communication and team development improvement reasons for holding the meeting. At the team briefing, any briefing information received from higher levels, in addition to material which has a specific relevance to that team, is presented for discussion and perhaps decision making. There are opportunities for the team members to raise questions or proposals relating to the team operations, or views to be passed upwards to the higher levels of management. The emphasis is on the 'local' (that is, team) use of the meeting time to deal with issues at the local level within a team situation. The team briefing leader is usually the team leader, a supervisor or manager who is in permanent and direct contact with the team.

The three-stage meeting process

Now you have decided not only that a meeting should be held, but also what type of meeting it is to be, you can proceed through the three major stages of meeting management:

- Preparation
- Implementation
- Post-meeting action

Or for those who like acronyms, PIP.

Of these three stages, as with most activities, the planning and preparation stage is often considered the most important. Without effective planning, the practice and implementation of any activity is almost doomed to failure. Planning and preparation are considered in this chapter and in Chapters 3 to 5; implementation will be discussed in Chapters 6 and 7; and post-meeting action in Chapter 8.

The planning will fall naturally into two aspects—people and things.

Preparation involving people

Who should be present?

It is an unfortunate fact of meetings that the people who should be present are not included and those who attend are not always the ones who should be there. It is up to you as a chairperson intent on producing an effective meeting to ensure that the meeting membership is the appropriate one.

You must recognize that people attend meetings for a number of personal or organizational reasons:

1 As a measure of their status in the organization.
2 As a measure of the status of their section/department in the organization.
3 To find out what is happening—whether or not it is relevant.
4 To obtain information about the subject.
5 To give information to the meeting.
6 To attend meetings for the sake of attending meetings.
7 To act as the boss's representative or substitute.
8 To try to impress another member or the chairperson.
9 Because he or she has always attended.
10 Because an invitation to attend was received.
11 To contribute effectively as a meeting member.

Apart from items 5, 7 and 11, attendance is not appropriate and people in other categories should be excluded. However, you must also take account of other pressures on you, e.g. is attendance non-appropriate because of pressure from management at a more senior level than you? Whether you should question membership in cases of this type will depend on your own power position in the organization, or perhaps your willingness to take risks.

Look at the members who form part of your meeting, who have been proposed as members or whom you are considering for membership and ask:

● Why should 'X' attend the meeting?
● Will they have an appropriate contribution to make?
● What would the effect be on the meeting or the subject(s) if they did not attend?
● Are there any other factors to be taken into account?

The danger of non-contributing members at a meeting is that the more there are of them the less smoothly the meeting is likely to run. Non-contributors can intimidate the 'real' members and their passivity can infect the other members. If their presence is unavoidable, it may be advantageous to have them seated apart from the contributing members, perhaps so that they are hardly visible.

Another area in which you may not have the final say is in the number of members, contributing or non-contributing, for the meeting. If the subject is complex, representatives from a number of disciplines may have to attend and consequently produce a large membership. There may be 'political' or 'Political' reasons why such and such a person, or such and such a number of persons should attend—if management has eight representatives, the trade unions will demand a similar representation, particularly if a vote is likely.

If there is a free choice, however, within the constraints of numbers imposed by the subject(s), research and experience suggest that a group of eight to ten is the optimum size for a meeting group, particularly where decisions have to be made. If the meeting is one simply of information giving, the meeting size need be constrained only by the physical aspects of the meeting room. The basic criterion is that if the meetings require effective contributions from the members, the greater the number of people present, the less time each has to contribute individually and there is always the possibility that excessive contribution time will be taken by the more articulate and dominant members. A large group is also a good environment in which people can hide, for whatever reason.

Length of stay at the meeting
In the majority of cases all the members will stay for the duration of a meeting. However, for multi-subject meetings it may be necessary for some experts or specialists to attend only for the part of the meeting that relates to them. This sounds simple to achieve, but is not necessarily so. You must decide whether the visitor stays for that relevant part of the meeting or for the whole meeting. If you invite the person to stay for the whole meeting, you must make it clear whether he or she can participate in the remainder of the meeting.

If the visitor is to attend for the particular part only of the meeting, he or she can either come at the start of the meeting in readiness for his or her spot, or come into the meeting as it proceeds. Attendance from the start can only be made economic for the visitor if the relevant part of the meeting is placed early on the agenda—this may or may not be possible.

Otherwise, accurate forecasting of timing and timing itself within the meeting are demanded and are not always possible. A compromise might be the solution in which a time is given for the representative to attend for his or her part of the meeting at an estimated ten minutes or so before that part is due to start. An explanation should be given of what is being arranged and why, and the warning given that the timing might not be exact. But you must try to ensure that the timing is achieved. It is a useful manoeuvre to have all the subjects requiring part-attenders to be early items on the agenda—the more into the meeting, the more likely there will be time slippage.

How long should the meeting last?

The effective use of time is paramount in the operation of a successful organization, and certainly in times of economic slow-down the relationship of time and money is important. The simple answer would be 'as long as it needs', but this might ignore a number of relevant and constricting factors. Your time may be restricted, the meeting room may be available only for a particular period and people have tasks requiring attention, people to meet elsewhere, etc., which restrict the time they have available to attend the meeting.

The attention span of people is restricted. Meetings lasting all morning or all afternoon, or even worse, all day, are much less likely to achieve effective results than short, impactive meetings.

If there is a lot of material to cover you should ask:

- Does all the material need to be covered in one meeting?
- Can the material be divided realistically into bundles of similar material?
- Can each 'bundle' be dealt with during a number of shorter and more impactive meetings? People often look more favourably on a number of shorter meetings than one marathon.

Guidance varies on the effective lengths of meetings, and it must be accepted that the subject must influence this considerably. A meeting of one hour's duration on a subject or connected series of subjects would appear to be an optimum, but circumstances will always dictate otherwise.

You can always take account of your knowledge of the members to decide the duration or other timing of the meeting. Senior managers have a higher cost-value on their time than junior managers and this must be taken into account. Some people are the owls or nightingales of this life—they come to life and attention when the day for most of us is coming to a close or even has finished. But conversely, in the mornings, when the 'larks' are active, the owls are sleepy and not at their mental and physical best. If you have a group of owls, it will be much more effective to delay the meeting until later in the morning or even the afternooon rather than hold it at the start of the day 'when everyone is fresh'! Unfortunately you may be the only one in this category! If you are forced into holding a meeting at a time when you know your group will not be as forthcoming as at other times, this is the occasion to keep the length of the meeting to a minimum—and let the members know of this intention at the start of the meeting.

Timing factors

The question of time is very important to the membership of meetings. It is the aspect of meetings most disliked by participants. Typical comments are: 'It was a good meeting in the early stages, but it just went on far too long. By the time it finished, I had opted out for a long time.' 'The meeting went on for so long, I started thinking about the work waiting for me.' 'Can I afford a day a week away from my work?'

Apart from the psychological factors of holding an over-long meeting, a failure to restrict the meeting effectively is inviting increased costs. The golden rules on timing include:

- Keep the meeting as short as possible bearing in mind the business to be achieved.
- If the number of items is likely to produce a very long meeting (more than an hour?), split the items into groups and hold more than one meeting.

You can usefully make determined efforts to discover from the members their views on the acceptable duration of meetings. A number of factors will naturally be involved:

- How significant for the person is the agenda
- How busy at the time the member may be

- How enjoyable the meetings are
- How well educated the member is in meeting participation
- The natural attention span of each member
- How important to the members' careers are
  —attendance at the meeting
  —the content of the agenda
  —the power position of the chairperson

The time allocation for meetings is obviously an important consideration for you during your meeting planning and, having determined how long the meeting should (will) last, this information must be transmitted to the members.

Two other aspects of timing must also be considered.

Starting times
You must ensure that the people essential to the meeting will be available and prepared—one aspect that it is often necessary to take into account is the incidence of shiftworking. A starting time for the meeting must be announced and you must keep to this decision (accidents excepted). You must consider very carefully whether to delay a meeting simply because some of the members have not yet appeared. In most cases the rule is 'start on time'.

If the meeting is delayed until all the latecomers arrive, the members who were there on time are being insulted—it is as if the chairperson was saying that the latecomers were more important than those who arrived on time. Eventually everybody will start arriving late 'because the meeting never starts on time'. However, a fetish must not be made of this starting time, because there will be occasions when a delay is unavoidable. For example, if a guest speaker who is first on the agenda has been delayed for a short while, it is only common sense to delay for that short period. However, if it becomes known that the speaker's delay will be considerable, some items of the agenda can be taken.

Do not fall into the trap of being your own delayer. If contact with the members is infrequent or difficult, it is easy for you to say 'Before we start, I just wanted to have a word with you Fred' because this has been the only opportunity to meet Fred. The result is that the start of the meeting is delayed by the chairperson, an unforgivable incident unless the 'word' with Fred is a matter of life or death.

Unless there are very good reasons for doing otherwise, when latecomers arrive, you should simply acknowledge the arrival and continue with the meeting. Otherwise, the 'late start' culture will develop with alienation of the supportive members.

Finishing times

Equally important as the starting time, though more difficult to control, is the finishing time for the meeting. With planning and preparation it should be possible to determine a realistic finishing time. Again this should be announced to the members at the start of the meeting or, preferably, on the notice of the meeting, and as far as possible should be adhered to.

Again do not let the finishing time become an overriding fetish as so many factors can get in the way. At the arrival of the stated finishing time, a revised assessment should be made of how much additional time is needed based on the importance of the remaining items. If further time is required, agreement for this should be sought from the members. Failure to act in a responsible manner in such circumstances will result in the attitude that 'our meetings never end on time' and attempts to avoid coming to the meeting will become more common.

One of the biggest time stealers is the inclusion of 'Any other business' in the agenda, or allowing members when the agreed agenda has been completed to bring up previously undeclared items.

Every effort should be made to exclude this from any meeting agenda. Obviously some emergency items can arise and these may have to be dealt with, but these should be rare. Otherwise you should develop a culture which requires the members arriving at the meeting with additional items to inform you before the start of the meeting. You can then decide whether the item warrants inclusion (and consequently additional time). Otherwise a meeting which was thought would last only half an hour can be extended considerably by several members clamouring to bring up urgent and important items.

The finishing time can also be linked with the occasion on which the meeting is held. There is less likely to be a voluntary, time wasting extension if the meeting is timed to finish at lunchtime or the end of the day. End of day at end of week can be even more effective, but you must always be aware of other effects which these timings might inject— members will not want to extend the meeting, but they may also inhibit themselves from a full discussion.

Chapter 3

Preparing for the meeting— the environment

Location of the meeting

You, or the organizer of the meeting, may or may not have any power of decision in deciding the location of the meeting. The meeting may be one held within an organization, and because of tradition or even the size of the membership, the meeting must be held in a particular room of the company building. But where the meeting is held can often be a major factor in determining the success or otherwise of a meeting.

Factors which might work against effectiveness will include:

- Too large and 'grand' a room
- Too small a room for division of the meeting into sub-groups
- Inaccessibility of the meeting room for all members
- Failure to inform security of visiting members

In addition you must ensure that

- hygiene factors are satisfied
  —air conditioning
  —fan noise
  —temperature control
  —toilet availability
  —natural lighting
  —comfortable seating
  —a visible clock
  —nearby provision of telephones
- administrative arrangements have been made
  —provision of refreshments
  —provision of paper and pens
  —visual aid equipment where necessary

—arrangements for urgent messages to be delayed
—availability of secretarial resources and fax machines

Requirements will vary with different meetings, so ensure that you and any support you may have, possess a complete and up-to-date checklist, similar to the one above, of items to be included in the preparation for the meeting.

Seating

The majority of meetings are held sitting down, therefore seating takes on an important aspect in the effectiveness of the meeting. The provision of comfortable seating has been mentioned above, but the arrangement of this seating can also have a major effect on the meeting.

You may, of course, have no opportunity of considering the seating. The seats may be fixed or impossible to move because of the nature of the room, but where variation is possible, you should always ask yourself whether the arrangement is the most appropriate for the particular situation. The more common arrangements are described below (see also Figure 3.1).

The theatre or classroom
When numbers are large, the traditional meeting seating arrangement is the theatre or classroom style, in which chairs are placed in rows in

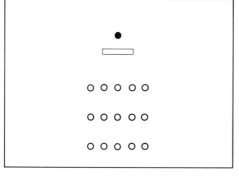

(a) classroom layout

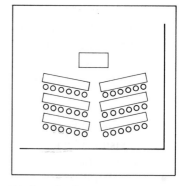

(b) herringbone

Figure 3.1   Seating arrangements

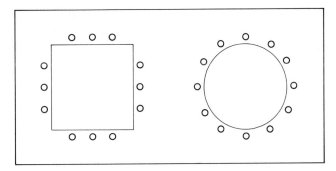

(c) boardroom

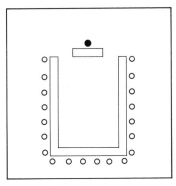

(d) U shape

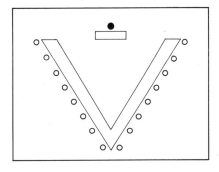

(e) V shape

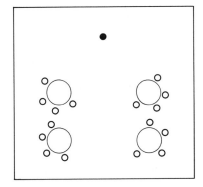

(f) clusters

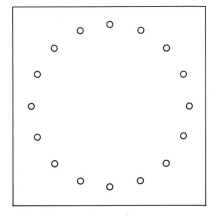

(g) circle

Figure 3.1   cont.

succession behind each other. The chairperson and, often, certain 'officers', are seated at a table placed at the front of the rows of seats, perhaps at a considerable distance from the furthest row.

Advantages
This arrangement has the advantage that the maximum number of people can be accommodated—but that is about the sole advantage.

Disadvantages
You will only be able to see clearly the front row—others will be only partly visible.

If the view is unimpeded, the view of individual members is that of the chairperson at the front, and the backs of the heads of the people in the row in front. Whenever anybody speaks, few are able to see the speaker and consequently effective listening is at a minimum.

The arrangement can be improved if each successive row is higher than the preceding one, as in many theatres or cinemas, but this improves only the sighting by and of the chairperson.

The herringbone
This variation of the theatre or classroom arrangement improves somewhat the visibility between members. The rows of seats, instead of all being carefully arranged so that everybody looks straight ahead and the rows are parallel to the front of the room, are in rows which are diagonally inclined. The outside of a row is nearer the front than the centre, thus producing an arrow shape pointing away from the front.

Advantages and disadvantages
There is some extra visibility between members, principally along a row, but there is still the problem of mainly seeing the backs of people's heads.

The boardroom
This is the traditional arrangement for small to medium sized meetings, one in which the members sit round the outside of a large table or number of tables placed together, with the chairperson at the 'head' of the table (a rectangular configuration will have two 'heads', but one will, often by tradition, be recognized as the chairperson's seat).

Advantages and disadvantages
The advantages are that most of the members are visible to each other and all are reasonably visible to the chair. There will be some difficulty in sighting people along the same side, so visibility is not complete. The table is useful for members to rest papers on, to write on and so on, but it can represent a barrier and in some situations can induce conflict with the people 'on the other side of the table'.

The open boardroom
The open boardroom seating arrangement is similar to the traditional boardroom, but instead of the table being solid, the constituent tables are moved outwards so that a well exists within the rectangle. Other members are able to sit in this well, thus increasing the size of the membership with a small increase only in floorspace.

Advantages and disadvantages
These are basically the same as for the boardroom but, although the configuration helps to provide extra places for members, the inter-visibility is not improved.

The U-shape
This is a layout in the shape of a U which can be used with or without tables in front of the members, the presence or absence depending on whether there will be a lot of writing and reference to papers, or whether the activity will be mainly verbal. The base of the U can be either rounded or squared-off. If tables are used, the members sit round the outside of the tables, rather like the boardroom layout, and again like the boardroom, if more members have to be accommodated they can sit at the inner sides of the tables, along the longer sides at least.

Advantages and disadvantages
Visibility between members is increased in this layout, although there are still some problems of visibility of members on the same side of the U and the 'conflict' position directly opposite the chair.

The V-shape
This is a natural development of the U shape, to try to avoid the two problems mentioned above. The seats are arranged in the form of a V rather than a U.

Advantages and disadvantages
The limitations of visibility along the side, although not completely eliminated, are reduced. If there is no seat at the point of the V, the opposing conflict position is also eliminated.

The circle
As the name suggests, the seats in this arrangement are in a circle facing towards the centre.

Advantages
Almost complete intervisibility is achieved, although there may be some problems with close neighbours depending on the size of the circle. The chairperson can be located anywhere around the circle and this can help to break down barriers if this is wanted.

A combination of the circle with the boardroom layout can enhance the latter. If the 'boardroom' table is circular instead of the traditional rectangle, a much less formal atmosphere is introduced and visibility is increased.

Clusters
Another informal and non-traditional form of seating for meetings places the members at small tables which are separated from each other and positioned in different parts of the room. The tables need not be geometrically placed, some degree of inclination to each other and the front of the room where the chairperson is located being possible. But the tables must be placed so that the narrow end of a rectangular table points in a forward direction. The members sit along the longer sides of the table and the short end faces forwards.

Advantages
Apart from breaking away from formality and tradition, this layout is helpful when small groups need to perform some activity or small-group discussion during the meeting—the small groups are already in existence at their 'family' tables.

Small, round tables can be used instead of rectangular ones, but in these cases some additional problems of visibility can develop if the seating positions are not carefully controlled.

Positioning members

Whether or not you have control over the seating arrangements also decides the control you have over where the members sit during the meeting. This positioning can often influence the effectiveness of a meeting.

In an ideal situation where all the members are fully functional, where they sit is not very relevant. If you have this atmosphere or one approaching it, it is simple to give the members completely free choice about where they sit. Friends will sit with friends, sectors will be made up of like members, early attenders will take seats away from the 'front', and so on.

However, sometimes it may be useful for you to decide where the members sit. For example, members who are to present items may be best placed near the front so that everybody has a chance of seeing them when it is their turn. In such cases, as in the case of the formal, official-type meeting, prepared nameplates can be used to determine where you want the members to sit.

If the meeting is part of a series, if the members are given a free choice, you will probably find that they choose the same seats on each occasion. This is linked with a safety factor—'this is my seat and I feel safe in it'. Similar considerations relate to pre-determined seating: if you determine where members are to sit, be consistent from one meeting to another as far as possible. If the members arrive and find that at each meeting their seats have been moved, you could be raising suspicion in addition to unease.

The dangers of free choice and 'clustering' include the greater likelihood of side-talking during the meeting—guidance is given later about how to deal with this, but perhaps avoidance is preferable to curative action.

Problem seats

If all your members are highly supportive of you, there are likely to be few or no problems about where people sit. But if there are possible problem members and there is a free choice of seating, you will find that the problem members tend to congregate in the seating arrangement furthest from you and directly opposite you—for example, in the boardroom seating, at the end of the table opposite you, or at the curve of the 'U' in that seating. This position has its parallels in the 'across the desk' conflict or formal position in negotiations or interviews. If you have control over the seating, place these members along the sides. This avoids their capability of being face on to you. It may not stop the conflict, but experience shows that it may help to reduce it. Conversely, when you require support during the meeting and you know you have members who will be active supporters, position them in this area and also, if possible, between potentially aggressive members along the sides. The principle of 'divide and conquer' helps somewhat, particularly in a large meeting.

When you are addressing the meeting or presenting information or proposals, you will be following good presentational skills practice by keeping eye contact with as many members as possible. This will be achieved by moving your direction of gaze around the members. Experience shows that when this is done, unless you are a very skilled presenter, you will tend to look in certain directions more than others.

This imbalance varies somewhat with different people but, for example, in a 'U' shaping, formal or informal, you are more likely to look at the people seated nearer the base of the 'U', the area away from you. The directly opposite position, the conflict position mentioned above, tends to be ignored—possibly to avoid the gaze of the possible aggressor. The nearest members, those at the extremities of the 'U', tend to be, usually unconsciously, ignored, perhaps because greater effort has to be made in turning your head. Consequently it will make good practice for you to look consciously at these extremity positions from time to time, otherwise the members there might feel they are being ignored.

Meeting costs

Cost must certainly be a consideration in planning the meeting and in the decision about how long it should last.

Cost of an hour long meeting
Attenders' hourly rate of £100 with 10 members = £1000.

(This of course would be a cost whether a meeting was being held or not.)

Opportunity cost (an amount related to what they would earn in production or service if they were not at the meeting) for the same group = £500. Total = £1500.

The opportunity rate, except when the members perform easily measurable tasks, is a difficult one to calculate, depending on many factors, objective and subjective. For the sake of example, the opportunity value has been taken as half their salary producing a total salary cost of £1500. If the meeting lasts for more than one hour, the cost increases roughly proportionally.

However, you must take other cost factors into account. These will include the following aspects:

- The cost of the meeting room (perhaps notional, but this may be relevant).
- The cost of the electricity and gas used when otherwise this would not be a factor.
- The cost of refreshments over and above what would otherwise be provided.
- The cost of time spent on preparation—both actual and opportunity time—for the chairperson and the members.
- The cost of such items used specifically in connection with the meeting and its results, e.g. stationery.
- The services of a minute clerk or secretary.
- Travelling costs if relevant, including the cost of such time.
- Miscellaneous lost time costs before and after the meeting.

It is almost impossible to assess all these factors accurately, and perhaps absolute accuracy may not be necessary, so a useful rule-of-thumb calculation can be total salaries plus 40 per cent.

However, the negative costs of the meeting must be balanced against more positive aspects. If a meeting has been held as has been agreed and the meeting is run effectively, there will be an end result with the achievement of the meeting objectives and consequently a saving of resources. The value of these achievements will be even more difficult to measure than the more specific costing ones, but they exist all the same.

Chapter 4

Planning the meeting

Objectives and agenda

The objectives for the meeting will decide the agenda in some cases, the agenda deciding the objectives in others. In a multi-subject meeting, there will be a number of items forming the agenda and each item will have its own objectives—some to discuss, some to recommend, some to decide, and so on. But a full planning of the meeting itself—the structure, the content, the behaviours, and so on—is essential.

Objectives

Whatever the type of meeting its objectives must be clear and comprehensive, based on the accepted criteria for objective setting:

- What has to be achieved by the end of the section or the meeting?
- That the objectives are clear, concise and understandable by everybody concerned.
- The reasons for raising the subject are fully known.
- By which time has the objective to be achieved?
- Who will be involved in the decision making and the implementation?
- How will the objective be achieved—during the meeting and in implementation?
- What other resources will be necessary?
- Where will any action take place?

But remember objectives are not set in stone. The meeting objectives set the terminal objectives for that meeting. During the process there will be incidents and new information which may have a bearing on the objectives. Notice must be taken of these and their effects taken into account. Consequently, although at the start of the journey you know where you are going and how you are going to get there, during the journey, to achieve this end, you may have to make several detours, some minor, some major.

You may find, as I have done on occasions, that a meeting which sets out as a simple information-giving or information-seeking process, may turn into, because of external or internal incidents, a full decision-making process.

Agenda
You are now in a position to produce your plan for the meeting from the objectives decided by you or for you; this plan is the agenda.

Very few meetings are held, or should be held, without an agenda of some sort. Where there is no agenda, particularly if there are a number of items to be considered and even more so if there is dominance, conflict or opposition during the meeting, these meetings are usually much less effective than those with an agenda. This effectiveness is still evident even when there is only one item for the meeting—for example the problem to be solved: benefits accrue from the statement of the problem being written down (having been defined or redefined) and posted so that all members can see it. These requirements of an agenda for a meeting and the benefits of it being written, are why written agendas are usually provided for members. And, of course, a filed set of agendas with any minutes or records that are made of the actual meeting form a record of the activity of that meeting group. However, there are occasions when an agenda is not required. Let us first consider this possibility.

No agenda
What happens if you do not have an agenda on normal occasions?

- Members may feel threatened because they usually have an agenda.
- Important items may be forgotten.
- Time will be spent on unimportant items because there is nothing to help in the control of the item action.
- Members attend without a full appreciation of what is to be achieved, and consequently may come unprepared.
- There will be no control or diminished control from the chair owing to
  —lack of confidence of the chairperson
  —absence of structure
  —uncertainty among the members.
- Members may not even turn up, believing that there is in fact nothing for the meeting to do, or the meeting is not sufficiently important for them to attend.

In a similar way, if you keep the agenda in your head, i.e. there is no written copy at all, the dangers are:

- You may forget some of the items to be covered.
- An ineffective structure may be followed.
- Confusion may exist among the members who will have come unprepared.

Some chairpersons follow a pattern of having an agenda, but they are the only ones with a copy; for some reason it is withheld from the members. There may be some justification for doing this on occasions, but you must consider very carefully the possible implications before copying this practice. There may be little support from the members who may feel that their membership is too unimportant to allow them into the 'secrets' of what is to happen in the meeting.

There is, however, justification on some occasions for you to hold a meeting without a written agenda or even advance notice to the members of the subject of the meeting.

Most people, when they have been invited to a meeting about which the subjects are known, come prepared with preconceived ideas, views, feelings and even proposals for action. If you find it is necessary for any of these attitudes to be changed, there is likely to be considerable resistance to the change from the preconceived position.

You can then consider the alternative approach of inviting relevant people to a meeting which will be described as one which will be concerned with solving a problem or making a decision. The subject is not announced, but it is essential that the reason for this action is made clear to the participants, namely that you want them to come with completely open minds about the subject.

Brainstorming meetings are often a useful occasion for this non-agenda issue, avoiding members attending with barriers to creativity produced by preconceived ideas.

In any situation when people are invited to a meeting without an agenda, you must have determined that they will not need to bring along with them any documentation. Otherwise, notice of what is required must be given.

Agenda guidelines

An agenda (although 'agenda' is the plural form of 'agendum' the latter is rarely used other than in a pedantic way) is a statement of the items which you intend to cover during the meeting. It is not only your working document but also one for the members attending the meeting. The agenda will normally be sent to the members in advance so that they might collect material relevant to the subjects.

Ideally the agenda will also indicate the action necessary for each of the agenda subjects and in total act as one of the most valuable resources for the meeting.

There are a number of guidelines for the use of an agenda which, if followed, can transform the agenda from a simple piece of paper to a useful document of help to both the members and the meeting. These include:

- The agenda should be in a written form.
- The written agenda should be circulated to the invited members sufficiently in advance of the meeting to allow/encourage them to consider the agenda items in advance, form some views, and ensure that they have any material or data to support the item and its discussion.
- The form of the written items should be sufficiently clear to enable members to know exactly what they mean and what is intended.
- The sequence of the written agenda items should, as far as possible, be that which will be followed at the meeting. (There will, of course, be occasions during a meeting when this sequence will have to be changed, but these occasions should be kept to a minimum.)

Agenda format

The format of written agendas can vary considerably from simple shopping lists to complex statements of intent. As in many situations, a midway, compromise position is usually the most effective.

The shopping list agenda

This is the simplest form of agenda, the type of 'agenda' which can often be found written on the back of an envelope! This suggests the level of importance that one can give to this type. An example of the simple shopping list agenda is given in Figure 4.1.

AGENDA FOR XXX MEETING TO BE HELD ON YYY

1 Minutes of last meeting

2 Financial statement

3 Purchase of equipment

4 Communication

5 European sales

6 Any other business

Figure 4.1 Simple shopping list agenda

The problem with the type of simple agenda in Figure 4.1 is that it is open to the widest misinterpretation.

1 *The minutes of the last meeting* What is going to be done with them? Have they been circulated? (Without this comment, members who have not received a copy cannot be certain that copies have or have not been circulated.) When was the last meeting? (If the minutes are not/ have not been circulated, members cannot be certain whether or not they have missed a meeting.)

2 *Items 2, 3, 4 and 5* What are these items going to be about? Is the financial statement just going to be discussed? Is it going to be analysed? Are there errors which have to be rectified? Is it intended that it should be agreed at the meeting? Are tasks to be allocated at the meeting?

Without a definition of what is intended by the item the danger is that various members will approach it with different interpretations. For example, item 3 might be seen as a decision not to purchase new equipment; or a decision to purchase; or a report on what has been purchased; or a policy statement relating to purchase, and so on. Depending on the interpretation by the member, relevant and necessary papers may not be brought to the meeting.

3 *Any other business* Although this item is usually included with the best of intentions to ensure that last minute, important items can be discussed, it is potentially the most dangerous item on the agenda.

Items for inclusion on the agenda should be sought from members when the agenda is being constructed. But as we have seen earlier, inclusion of an item on the agenda gives notice to everybody of intended action. A member may not want the chairperson or the other members to be prepared for what he or she intends to introduce, and consequently does not give advance notice, springing the item under 'Any other business'. The safest and most effective action is not to have this type of agenda item and to consider at the meeting those items only which have been given prior notice. Of course, there will be occasions when something urgent and important arises which has to be included in the meeting—such an item does not need an 'Any other business' agenda item for the chairperson to decide whether it justifies inclusion.

At best it can be said that a shopping list of this nature is better than no agenda at all when an agenda is necessary.

The extended shopping list

The value of the simple shopping list agenda can be improved by simple additions to the listing. A modified version of the example could appear as shown in Figure 4.2.

AGENDA FOR XXX MEETING TO BE HELD ON YYY

1 Circulated minutes of the meeting held on XXX to be confirmed.

2 Report on and make further decisions on matters arising from the minutes, in particular 6/1992 action relating to the annual sales conference and 12/1992 report on action taken to reduce wastage in production centre.

3 Receive, discuss and confirm the financial statement.

4 Decide on the purchase of new equipment for the additional production area.

5 Discuss and agree methods of improving internal telephone communication methods.

6 Recommend methods to improve European sales.

7 Agree date and time of next meeting.

Figure 4.2   Extended shopping list agenda

If you provide an agenda of this nature, the members will at least know what is going to happen with each agenda item, have the opportunity to read any papers relating to the subjects, make their own investigations of current practice (e.g. item 5) and collect material which will be used during the meeting.

The effective agenda

What to include in the agenda

You will be tempted to include any items that you feel need clarification and consultation, but unfortunately this on so many occasions means a long agenda when there is really insufficient time to deal with each item effectively and to deal with all the items. You must try to assess how long each item will take to reach a satisfactory conclusion and include only those which can be contained within the agreed length of the meeting. You will also find that it is useful to have an inbuilt extension for each major item in case you have to cover a longer discussion than you envisage. If the failure to complete the agenda becomes a regular feature, the agenda as an important document will fall into disrepute among the members with negative results.

Therefore, you should construct the agenda on the following priority basis:

- The important items which must be decided during the meeting.
- Some time for the minor items as buffers.
- Some discontinuity time.

In many cases this means that not everything can be included on the agenda. Consider the items which you would like to include but which may have to be omitted and question:

- Does it need to be included?
- Why does it have to be included?
- What would be the result if it was not included? Would there be serious implications?
- Does every item need to be discussed at that meeting?
- Can the item(s) be covered in ways other than at a meeting?

In this way you may be able to reduce the number of agenda items to manageable proportions using these criteria. But there will be occasions when the number of agenda items and the realistic time needed outweigh the time available at the meeting at which they must be raised. In such a case, you will have no alternative to extending the time of the meeting, however unacceptable this might be. But before deciding on this approach, you must reconsider all your proposed agenda items to see whether

- the item's inclusion is essential,
- the item is being included because it is one of your favourite subjects,
- the item is a popular subject among the members,
- you are being pressured from elsewhere to include the item which may not be essential (you must try then to reduce the pressure and obtain agreement to delayed discussion of the item).

If extension beyond the normal cannot be avoided, and the organization or group culture might be antagonized, the progress of the meeting might suffer through member attitudes. In such cases the chairperson must perform a significant 'selling' job on the essential reasons for extending the meeting.

Any other business (AOB)
It appears to have been almost a tradition to complete every agenda and meeting with 'Any other business', the invitation for any member to raise any type of matter at all, whether or not it has anything to do with the current business of the meeting. As a result, meetings have been known to continue longer with AOB than with the business laid down in the agenda. Inclusion of this item will be the major invitation to extend the length of the meeting and deny the stated finishing time.

When you are preparing the agenda, this task should not be yours alone. There will be items that the chairperson wishes to include in the meeting—these are the principal *raisons d'être* for the meeting. But before the agenda is finalized, all the members should be asked if they wish to contribute items for the agenda.

Any who wish to do so should be asked to provide the following:

- An agenda item title
- A short description of the item
- A statement of the objectives of the item
- A comment on how important the item is to the organization, the meeting group and individual
- An estimate of the time needed to cover the item

You will be the one who usually decides whether an item should be included in the agenda or whether it should be referred back to the originator for reconsideration or broadcast by some other means. Member items should, however, only be rejected or returned if it is impossible to give them a higher priority than items already entered.

The chairperson's items, supplemented by those of the members, should be sufficient for the meeting agenda. Consequently, there should never be an item entitled 'Any other business'. This encourages members not to bother to give prior warning of interests and can easily sabotage the timing of the meeting.

As mentioned earlier there will be, of course, occasions at a meeting when a member has an important and urgent item that must be raised and *which has only recently arisen*. It may be that immediately prior to attending the meeting the member learned of something which was relevant to the meeting membership but was not covered on the agenda and which needed urgent discussion. In this case, the chairperson would probably agree to discussion, etc.

What chairpersons should encourage, however, is notification by the members at the beginning of the meeting if they have an item of this nature. The chairperson can then decide whether it is relevant to add it to the actual agenda.

Even if there is no AOB item on the agenda, many chairpersons feel obliged to ask at the end of the official agenda whether there is anything else. You must resist any temptation to do this. Stick to the published agenda and eventually the members will realize that this is what you intend and will help to develop the meeting culture you are trying to build.

Therefore, you should educate your meeting members to

- contribute agenda items prior to the meeting to the agenda,
- discuss an AOB item at the start of the meeting if this is urgent and important,
- bring up additional items without prior warning in the case of an emergency only.

You should

- seek to involve the members in the construction of the agenda,
- exclude any reference to AOB on your agendas,

- not seek additional items at the end of the meeting,
- develop a culture (apart from emergency and really urgent items) of using the agenda as the limits of the meeting and consequently keeping within the published meeting duration.

Position of items on the agenda
The positioning of any item on the agenda may be controlled by its importance, its popularity with you and/or the members, the time required for its discussion, the presence of a visitor presenting a subject, the organizational culture, tradition and custom or, sometimes, even logical assessment. Any of these can dictate position, but some may make the progress of a meeting more difficult.

The formality of the agenda will decide the position of some of the items. For example, in the case of formal, official meetings, minutes of the previous meeting may have been circulated to members and it will therefore be necessary to have these confirmed at an early stage. If the draft minutes have been circulated and the members given an opportunity to suggest amendments, little time will be taken up in their confirmation.

Similarly, a common agenda item is concerned with apologies for absence. This can be cleared speedily early in the agenda.

Items of minor importance
Problems start occurring when the major items of the agenda are being considered for ordering. There is often the tendency to consider the least important agenda items and list these to be held at the start of the meeting as they will be speedily processed.

Several problems arise with this attitude. If the items are of very minor importance, why are they included in the meeting? Is it not possible for them to be dealt with in an alternative way and therefore not even appear on the agenda? If they have to be considered at the meeting, although they are of low importance, early in the meeting is a useful time to deal with them, provided that

- a realistic time bounding has been decided by the chairperson,
- this time allocation is controlled and strictly adhered to,
- any latecomers will miss only these less important items.

There is always a very strong temptation with minor matters to spend too long in discussion, often because the chairperson and members are procrastinating so that they can delay the difficult item further in the agenda. Also, of course, as mentioned earlier, if excessive time is used on these items, time for really important items will be more restricted. If, however, there is no problem in control, clearing the minor matters first can be an effective strategy.

Important items
The next item on the agenda will normally be the most important item. If it is so important it deserves this early position so that a realistic time allocation can be given to it. If discussion takes longer than forecast and the meeting has to terminate before the end of the agreed time, at least this most important item will have been dealt with.

Consequently, it may be a useful strategy to have one or two minor items at the end of the agenda as well as at the beginning, so that little is lost if there is not time to deal with them.

Remember earlier mention of the characteristics of members, particularly the ones with larks' and owls' syndromes. If it is necessary, you can use these factors to control or even manipulate the agenda. If you place important items late on an agenda of a meeting which is held close to lunchtime or the end of the day, they are less likely to receive the consideration they deserve. Consequently you may wish to include the most important item first on the agenda, ignoring the possibility of any latecomers.

But some chairpersons have used item placing in order to manipulate discussion. If a controversial item is left to the end of the agenda, conflict might be avoided because the members will only be interested in leaving the meeting. This is a dangerous tactic, because the members may realize either the strategy or the importance of the item and in the first case decide to play the same game or otherwise control their impatience to leave!

An alternative agenda

There is every likelihood that the agenda will be an effective meeting document for both you and the members if it contains as much prior information about the items as possible. We have already seen how the shopping list can be developed into a more useful instrument. Further improvements are possible.

The traditional role of the chairperson is to introduce the agenda item and lead and control the discussion on the subject, take proposals and enable decision making, summarize the agreements and take part in the discussions. This is asking a considerable amount of the chairperson whose control function may not be easy.

The alternative approach, often more acceptable to the membership, is for the people who are most appropriate to introduce a subject, lead the discussion and otherwise take responsibility for the subject. This person might be the chairperson, but could easily be any other member(s). In such instances you as chairperson are given more space in which to control and support the discussion. Even the item summary can be undertaken by the lead member and you maintain an overall sight of the process, ensuring that it is conducted with full effectiveness. This more effective method of holding a meeting can be reflected in the agenda. An agenda of this type would include the following:

- A full description of the item
- A statement of the objectives—discussion, consideration, decision making, recommendation, etc.
- A detailing of the member responsible for the item
- A listing of material relating to the item that the members will need to bring with them (e.g. papers previously circulated)

With information of this nature given to members, there is wider awareness before the meeting of what is likely to occur and who is responsible. Contact can be made with the lead member and questions resolved before the meeting, rather than taking up time at the meeting itself.

Some chairpersons also append a note about the timing of the item, the durations having been decided by the importance and complexity of the item. This is a very difficult aspect of agenda and meeting construction and should only be attempted if you are very experienced and skilled at meeting management. Posting to the agenda gives the duration a possibly restrictive atmosphere and estimates may fall into ridicule if they are always wrong. Certainly you should include timing and item duration in your pre-meeting consideration, but entry on the agenda may be omitted. Figures 4.3 and 4.4 suggest some possible formats for extended agendas of this nature.

FORM FOR MEETING AGENDA (A)

1 NAME OF MEETING ....

2 DATE ....

3 STARTING TIME .... FINISHING TIME PLANNED ....

4 LOCATION ....

5 PEOPLE INVITED

....|

   |..|

....|

   |..|

....|

   |..|

....|

   |..|

6 _____

No.	Agenda item	Who responsible	Action agreed
(1)			
(2)			
(3)			

_____ and so on.

7 MATERIALS. PAPERS REQUIRED

....

....

....

NOTES

....

....

....

Figure 4.3 A recommended full agenda format

MEETING ....DATE..

STARTING TIME ....FINISHING TIME ....

DETAILS OF LOCATION ....

PURPOSE OR DESIRED OUTCOME OF MEETING

....

Timing	Agenda item	Method of presentation	Who responsible	Equipment/ material	Action	Follow-up

Figure 4.4 An alternative full agenda format

Chapter 5

Final arrangements

By this stage you will have considered the items to include on the agenda—in whatever form decided. You will have taken action on the physical and administrative aspects relating to the meeting and you are almost ready for the meeting. There are one or two additional tasks before you launch into the meeting. One—an expectations assessment—may appear to be a luxury although once you have tried it you will realize that it is not. The others are essential parts of the meeting process.

Agenda analysis

On so many occasions we enter a process of some nature and find within a short period of time that things are not going right. An immediate assessment is made of the problems and in most cases the thought is 'I'd have realized that this would happen if I'd only thought about it earlier.'

You have little excuse to make this statement if things start to go wrong in your meeting. Part of your pre-meeting preparation is an analysis of the agenda items with an in-depth consideration of them. During this assessment you will be considering the items in terms of the level of their acceptability to you, to the meeting membership as a whole, or perhaps to factions of that membership. This division into 'sides' is particularly evident in meetings which have statutory representatives from management, trade union or other factions. Internally you might be faced with the sales staff versus the production staff; the shop floor versus the office staff, and so on. There are few meetings, other than perhaps team meetings, where everybody is on the one side!

During the meeting proposals may come from one side, only to raise conflict or aggression in the other side(s); arguments may flare about even the most apparently innocuous statement or event; sides may range against each other with the result that deadlock is approached.

It is in these situations that the pre-meeting, agenda analysis can be very helpful and give you an opportunity:

- To identify the problem areas.
- To assess their significance.
- To identify their locations.
- To consider methods of approaching them during the meeting.

This may have the appearance of looking for problems where they might not exist. They might not exist, but if they do and they appear during the meeting, you have prepared yourself for them as well as you can. This must improve your chances of success.

Agenda analysis method
1 Divide a piece of paper with a vertical line: one side should be headed 'My views' and the other side 'Members' views'.
2 On the 'My views' side, list all the agenda items and the separate major parts of each item if this is relevant. For example, the item 'To agree the monthly bonus' might be made up of
   (i)   the basis for producing the figures
   (ii) comparison with previous months
   (iii) conclusions to be drawn
   (iv) agreement to be reached.
3 Consider carefully each item and sub-item. If you feel that the item or sub-item will be accepted readily, annotate the entry with a tick ($\checkmark$). If, however, you feel that the members or a political group within the membership will argue strongly against, disagree with or generally not accept the item, annotate with a cross (X). (If the disagreement, etc., is likely to be violent or extreme, an XX entry can be used!)
4 The next step, which will be much less concrete in its conclusions, is to list, on the other half of the paper, the issues—as part of the agenda items or associated issues, or completely separate issues which are likely to be raised—which you consider the members are likely to raise. The pointers to these issues will be comments you have heard in various ways, direct reports to you, previous actions, or your own suspicions about what is going on. This assessment, of course, is much less certain than the listing of the agenda items because many of these issues will represent the infamous 'hidden agenda'.
5 When you have listed these potential issues to be raised by the others, consider them very carefully and try to assess your actual or likely attitudes to the issues. If you can, or are likely to accept them readily, place a $\checkmark$ against them. If you feel that you, your supporters or some of the other members will need to argue against them, or they will be rejected with non-acceptance of the rejection, place a X (or XX!).

6 The completed assessment sheet will, almost at a glance, give you both a general, overall view and a detailed assessment of the likely nature of the meeting. The greater the number of Xs, the more difficult the meeting is likely to be. You will have an indication of where the problems will fall and this will give you an opportunity to consider how you might approach having to deal with the situation.

A similar approach can be taken when there are two potentially opposing sides in the meeting. Instead of assessing 'you' and 'them', your analysis will be 'them 1' and 'them 2'.

An analysis of this nature obviously does not resolve the problems, but with its indication of the problems and the accompanying assessment and analysis, thought will have been given to them and plans made accordingly. This is obviously much more effective than being presented with problems on the spot and having to try to deal with them without the benefit of preparation.

Successful reaction to an item might not be obvious in every case, but only pre-meeting analysis may suggest that it is possible. Consequently you are warned to consider what action to take.

Table 5.1   Part of meeting preparation chart

Item: To agree monthly bonus			
My views		Members' views	
1. Basis for producing figures	✓		X
2. Comparison with previous months	✓		✓
3. Conclusions to be drawn	✓		X
4. Agreement to be reached	X		X
5.	X	Demand for 5% increase in bonus	✓
6.	✓	Earlier payment of bonus	✓

Table 5.1 suggests a format which might be adopted for an agenda analysis.

Final pre-meeting tasks

All that remains for you now to confirm before the meeting itself are items of administration to ensure that the meeting runs smoothly. These can include the following:

- Sending out the formal notice of the meeting.
- Confirming the physical arrangements.
- Considering other aspects of the meeting to which you have so far not given thought, e.g. how formal the meeting is to be; how decisions are to be made; and for post-meeting action, how decisions are going to be recorded and implemented.

Formal notices

Unless you are a completely new chairperson and the meeting you are to hold is the first of its kind, the members will already have some indications of the forthcoming meeting. Hopefully you will have invited them to contribute to the agenda or a date of the meeting was set at the previous meeting. But it is necessary to take certain formal action to ensure that everybody is fully aware of the coming meeting. After all, some members may have been on holiday or sick absence, or there may be one or two new members with whom there has been no contact.

As soon as the meeting date is fixed, a short note should be sent to all members informing them of the date, time and, if possible, location of the meeting. This will also be the occasion to seek items for the agenda, always giving a final date by which submissions should be made.

The next stage will be the issue of the agenda. This will confirm the date, time and location and it is usual to send with the agenda any relevant papers or reports which will be considered at the meeting. This indicates that the agenda should be sent out as far in advance of the meeting as possible to give the members time to assimilate the papers and obtain their own information. Two weeks is a usual and useful period before the meeting. If any papers are delayed, they must be sent to the members as soon as they become available, avoiding if possible having to issue them at the meeting. In this latter case, there will be no time for the members to read the paper and give it justice; reliance will then have to be placed on a substantial presentation of the paper by its author—the utilization of more time than the meeting can usually afford.

Nor should the agenda and its accompanying items be sent out only a day or so before the meeting. The members must have time to make their preparations rather than have to admit that they had insufficient time to prepare.

You may have some support in your administrative tasks related to the meeting. I would certainly suggest that even if you have support, you keep a personal watch on the sending of the agenda, etc. This will avoid comments by the members of lack of completeness of their meeting package. However, ensure that when you attend the meeting, spare copies of the agenda and all papers are available for members who either claim they haven't received them or have mislaid them.

Confirmation of the meeting environment

You have previously made arrangements for the room and the necessary stationery, equipment and services, but you would be wise to check, or have checked by your support, shortly before the meeting whether there have been any changes. If your arrangements were made some time previously, anything could have happened in the interim without your being advised.

Personal checklist

In order to help you to make arrangements and then to check these at a later date, you will find a personal checklist invaluable. Even when you are accustomed to taking all the action, the checklist can ensure that familiarity will not allow omissions.

Table 5.2 is a specimen checklist: it may not be completely relevant in your case—delete the items which do not refer to you and make your own personal additions. Time given to producing a comprehensive list will pay dividends for you in the future and will require only minimum maintenance.

Table 5.2 Specimen checklist

Action	Who is responsible	By when
(a) Pre-meeting arrangements		
Notifications		
Consideration whether to hold a meeting	....	....
Advance notices sent—to whom	....	....
Requests for agenda items sent —to whom	....	....
Requests for reports	....	....
Agenda		
Collation of member agenda items	....	....
Completion of agenda	....	....
Previous minutes/action notes	....	....
Collation of reports	....	....
Other related resources—guests, etc.	....	....
Assignments		
Delegation of tasks	....	....
Arrangement for secretarial assistance	....	....
Arrangements for presenters in lead items	....	....

(b) Pre-meeting checklist

	Checked
Environmental check	
Meeting room booked	....
Access method	....
Electrical sockets needed	....
Suitability of room for event	....
Other required rooms available	....
Parking facilities	....
Porterage access	....
Seating arrangements	....

Action	*Checked*
Sufficient chairs, tables, etc.	....
Toilets locations and availability	....
Telephone access	....
Fax availability	....
Clerical/secretarial contact	....
Lighting control	....
Wall space for posters, etc.	....
Cleanliness	....
Ventilation regulation	....
Refreshment availability	....
Refreshments ordered	....
Photocopier availability	....
Posters, screen shots visible	....

Equipment check

Audio recorder and tapes	....
Video recorder, monitor and tapes	....
Directional signs as necessary	....
Extension cords	....
Microphones	....
Overhead projector	....
Flipchart and stand	....
Film projector and screen	....
Slide projector and screen	....
Lectern	....
Whiteboard and wiper	....

Materials check

Nameplates	....
Blotter pads	....
Small felt tip pens or similar	....
Large felt tip pens or similar	....
Drymarker pens	....
Lumocolour pens—water and spirit based	....
Highlighter pens	....
Acetate sheets and rolls	....
Pencils	....

Action	Checked
Masking tape	....
Blutack	....
Paper clips	....
Scissors	....
Stapler	....
Hole punch	....
Flipchart paper	....
A4 lined/plain paper	....
File folders	....
Clipboards	....
Reference books	....
Visual aids	....
Water carafes and glasses	....
Bottled water, juices, etc.	....
Bowls of sweets, etc.	....
Copies of papers and reports	....
Copies of agenda	....
File of previous minutes	....

Immediately before meeting

Check all seating, tables, extra seating available	....
Check all other rooms available	....
Check equipment available and working	....
Check refreshments—water and other supply available	....
Own agenda and other resources available	....
Spare copies of agenda, papers, etc., available	....
Apologies received	....
Confirm guests coming	....
Secretarial assistance available	....
Clock available, working and correct	....

Apart from decisions concerned with the way you are to behave at the meeting, present yourself and your role, you should now be ready for the meeting itself. However, the way you behave as chairperson is so vital to the success of the meeting, the next chapter will be devoted to this subject.

Chapter 6

Chairperson behaviour

In the majority of cases the success and achievement of a meeting depend on the skill of the chairperson to arrange, organize, implement and control the process. Much of the activity by you will be with the people who make up the membership of the meeting. You will need to relate to them to the extent that their information, knowledge and skills are brought to bear on the problems raised in the meeting. To do this you will have to practise all the behavioural skills you can muster. These skills will include not only the manner in which you come over to and consequently are accepted or rejected by the others, but also how you deal with the members—the supportive ones and the more difficult ones. These skills are the principal ones required by a chairperson. You will not always succeed, but awareness of the requirements of your role will ensure that at least you attempt to relate to the members and this attempt is recognized by them.

Chairperson styles

What sort of chairperson are you going to be? This aspect is complicated by the fact that the behaviour of people, planned or not, can conflict with the specific requirements of different meeting. There is no such person as the 'ideal chairperson', rather this role is approached by a skilled chairperson behaving in the manner most appropriate for each situation. A tall order!

Meeting variations

We have seen earlier that there are different types of meetings with their own particular structures. These structures also require the chairperson to behave in ways appropriate to these different needs.

Information-giving meetings
If you are holding an information-giving meeting, during the earlier

stages you will be presenting the information to the members. This stage requires you to be a good presenter, articulate, using the language and techniques appropriate to the audience and the situation, and above all interested in ensuring that the listeners understand your message. You must have understanding of the different ways that people listen and understand information and possess the skills of identifying the extent of this understanding, perhaps by being aware of the non-verbal signals being given.

You can, at the very least, check directly with the audience at intervals that they have understood, simply by asking them, or in certain circumstances setting some form of test. This means that you will have to break your material down into digestible bits which are specifically capable of being checked before moving on to the next. It is not sufficient to ask 'Do you all understand that?' because in many circumstances in a group, few people will admit their non-understanding. More specific questions must be formulated, depending on the subject being presented.

At the end of the information-giving section a complete change of behaviour must be made so that when the members are asking questions, giving their views, and responding to the questions you may be asking to test their understanding, you are in a listening rather than telling mode. You must be able to listen carefully to their views and questions and respond as openly as possible to the latter, rather than use this time as an opportunity for a further monologue.

Information-seeking meetings

In this type of meeting your behaviour must be concentrated in the ways described for the end of the information-giving meeting, but even more skilfully expressed. Your questioning techniques must be well planned so that you obtain useful responses rather than closed ones or even silence. An essential aspect of this meeting is to question in a way that does not appear to be cross-examination and that, not only are you interested in the members' views, but you are seeking the information for realistic reasons.

Questioning has limitations on occasions and you must have some knowledge of techniques which you can employ to obtain information if it is not easily forthcoming. Buzz groups are usually effective approaches when the members, although they have information and views, have reservations about expressing these openly in what may be a group of strangers.

Listening skills are all important and the listening must be active, demonstrating overtly that you are doing so and that views, however badly formed or naïve, will still be listened to and taken into account by you.

Decision-making meetings

Behaviour becomes a much more difficult application in this type of meeting, particularly when it is multi-subject. Decision-making meetings must be seen to be (and be) events called for the members to take part in the decision-making process and not, as can happen, be rubber-stamp events.

In this type of meeting one agenda item may be information giving; another information seeking; another seeking commitment to implementing a solved problem; one in which you present a proposal and lead a discussion yourself or one in which you hand over most of the lead to a member for a subject. All these situations occurring within one meeting demand a frequent switch of behaviour and you must be able to do this in order to be an effective chairperson.

Changing behaviour to suit a situation is not changing yourself and your personality: it is merely acting in a manner that is appropriate to the situation. We are already doing this, sometimes consciously, at other times unconsciously. The manager at work is often a 'different' person at home with the family; a 'different' person in the pub with a group of friends; a 'different' person standing screaming at a local derby football match; a 'different' person sitting in front of a promotion or selection panel, and so on. We all play many parts and frequently we know that we have to change our part (behaviour) to succeed in the new situation. The same applies to the chairperson who might have to chair many different kinds of meeting.

Consultative meetings

The other principal type of meeting we identified earlier was the general or consultative type of meeting where the objective is for the membership to discuss a topic or topics and perhaps come to their own decisions. In such a case, the chairperson ceases to have that more formal role and becomes a group discussion leader, introducing the subject, ensuring that everybody knows what it is, then encouraging the members to talk and discuss. The behaviour that is most inappropriate in such a situation is for the chairperson to be the major contributor, forcing his or her views and discouraging the members from making their points known. But the chairperson does not just throw the subject in and sit back to daydream; while the group is discussing he or she will be listening intently, perhaps posing a probing question if a loose statement is allowed to pass; but above all storing up the views to give a comprehensive summary at the end of the meeting.

Some people are obviously more capable of switching behaviours than others; the ones who find it difficult or feel that they are unable to do so, must practise if they are to increase their meeting management effectiveness.

Decision-making processes

Many meetings involve decision making within the meeting and you will have to identify aspects of this process within your chairperson behavioural style. The membership of the meeting must also be clear about how decisions are to be made within defined parameters.

The process may be defined by the culture or procedural instructions of the organization; by the personal decision of the chairperson; but preferably, where it is organizationally feasible, by the group of people who are to take decisions. If the process has been laid down by tradition or by the organization, you must, at an early stage in the life of the meeting group, let them know this. Otherwise it is very useful to include as an early item of the first meeting: 'To discuss and agree a method by which this meeting group will reach decisions where there is some form of disagreement in the group.'

Decisions are made in a variety of ways.

1 *Singular or autocratic* Here the chairperson either makes the decision following discussion by the meeting, or acts as the final arbiter.
2 *Majority decision* A common, popular but not always the most appropriate or effective method. Even though the members might have agreed to this approach (although usually it is imposed), the ones in the losing minority can continue to nurse a preference for their own views or even a grievance that they had lost.
3 *Unanimity* When this happens there are no problems, but the astute chairperson should be aware of all the signals which confirm unanimity rather than some members not agreeing, but saying nothing.
4 *Consensus* Often misinterpreted as 'majority decision', the ideal of this decision approach should be unanimity, perhaps after a discussion

brought about by initial disagreements. Following discussion, influencing by argument and winning over either minority or majority factions to one side, all the members agree to agree on the action.

5 *Compromise* This method approaches that of consensus, but in this case there may be some members at the end of the discussion who still do not agree, *but they have entered a definite commitment that even if they do not agree they will support the decision.* The latter part of this statement is quite different from a commonly made statement 'OK, I'll go along with it' usually said in the spirit of 'I'll go along with it because I have to, not because I want to, and I shall either continue to get my own way or try to sabotage the decision.'

Compromise or apparent consensus which has to be hard fought is an uneasy bedfellow because people are frequently left with the feeling that this acceptance is only superficial.

Unanimity is the ideal, imposition is the antithesis (although sometimes the norm). Consensus is an achievable ideal which should be striven for, although compromise frequently has to be accepted. Majority decision is the most commonly used approach, but is not necessarily the most effective in spite of this.

Where influence is a factor in the decision-making process, both chairperson and members should be aware of any attempts to influence decisions or have them made by a vocal majority or vocal minority. In the former, although their case may not be the most effective or appropriate, a decision is forced in that direction by the sheer strength of articulation, voice power, inappropriate behaviour by that vocal majority. One consolation (if indeed it can be described as such) is that if a majority vote had to be taken the view would be carried. In the case of the vocal minority this is much more dangerous, because it tends towards domination of people by a small group of people who use their power— personality, dominant behaviours, pressured articulation, loud presentations and so on—to subdue the opposition, albeit a majority.

Leadership styles

In the simplest of terms, chairpersons or leaders fall into three main categories—*managers, facilitators* and *controllers*. If you are to make the most of yourself as a chairperson, it is necessary to consider into which category or categories you fall, how much use you make of categories which are not your norm, and how flexible you are in using the category style appropriate to the situation.

The manager

Basically the manager is there to see that the members perform in the required manner and produce the required results, although in many cases the manager sees himself or herself as the only one with the knowledge, skill and expertise to make an effective decision. The biggest problem encountered is ensuring that the membership accept this state of affairs and the solutions produced (or perhaps the manager might even accept a modification of it). This act of ensuring effective working can often require the chairperson to act as a 'boss' in the narrowest sense of this word.

There are occasions when this approach is appropriate, although perhaps not necessarily the most appropriate. When a group of members who are inexperienced or unskilled, or both, are drawn together, they need strong leadership in the early stages to help them start to knit together—the 'manager' will help in this process. But he or she must also be aware of the time to modify this behaviour as the group starts to weld into a team. Unfortunately, only too frequently the 'manager' continues as he or she has started and the people development is lost.

The facilitator

The facilitator is quite the reverse, seeing himself or herself as the encourager of the members. He or she is very interested in the process of the development of the members into a working team, capable of solving problems and making decisions with the minimum of intervention. The facilitator takes a back seat once the action has been set in motion, encouraging the members by his or her presence but letting them move forward themselves. He or she can sometimes intervene if the process seems to be going badly wrong, or if suggestions based on experience are required—these, however, will be presented not as 'thou shalt', but rather as 'what do you think about the idea of doing . . .?'

The controller

The controller looks at the people process, encouraging the quiet members, holding back the overactive, separating the fighters, and so on. If there are rules or procedures for the conduct of the meeting, the controller sees his or her role as ensuring that these are followed (slavishly in extreme cases) and may need to keep order to ensure this.

(The Speaker of the House of Commons is the archetype of controllers with her most frequently used words 'Order, Order!') One of the major advantages of the controller is that during the meeting all members are treated fairly and as equally as possible. Power groups can easily dominate the group and the facilitator, and every group is subsumed by the manager. But the controller has time to observe the contribution pattern and bring in the quieter members.

At the extreme of being the controller of procedures, this role is usually limited to statutory bodies—Parliament, local councils, some shareholder meetings. At the other pole, such a chairperson can have a very beneficial effect of helping a meeting of varied people run more smoothly than other chairpersons.

One advantage of the controller role is that, if the controlling skill is held by the individual, he or she need have no knowledge of the subjects under discussion. His or her skill comes in controlling and guiding meetings. I was placed in this position some years ago when, newly elected to the parish council, knowing nothing about council procedures, etc., I was elected chairman at my first meeting (possibly because the other members were aware of my experience in the chair with other organizations). For the first few meetings, until I learned what 'penny rates' and 'precepts' were, I concentrated on managing the meetings.

We like to think that we take on all three roles at the relevant times, but observation shows that this is not always so and that many of us have a predilection towards one particular style. If this is so, then this is the recipe for problems arising. If we are by nature and preference a facilitator, but the situation in a meeting requires that we take control, ensure that people do things, perhaps tell them what to do and otherwise be the 'boss' of the situation, we are less likely to move easily to that role. And vice versa.

The chairperson of a meeting, like the leader of many other types of work groups, has two forces to balance—ensuring that the task is performed, and ensuring that all the members have equal opportunities and are effective members. These requirements can easily get out of balance. The range of variations can be summarized by a modification of the leadership continuum of Tannenbaum and Schmidt (1973). On the diagram shown in Figure 6.1 the direct involvement, authority and area of freedom of the members increases with a corresponding decrease in the authoritative approach of the chairperson.

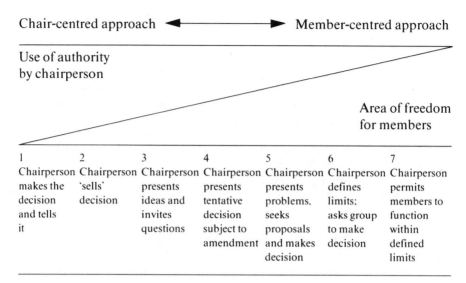

| Chair-centred approach ◄————————► Member-centred approach |

1	2	3	4	5	6	7
Chairperson makes the decision and tells it	Chairperson 'sells' decision	Chairperson presents ideas and invites questions	Chairperson presents tentative decision subject to amendment	Chairperson presents problems, seeks proposals and makes decision	Chairperson defines limits; asks group to make decision	Chairperson permits members to function within defined limits

Figure 6.1 The chairperson continuum

Behaviour awareness

If you are to behave in the most appropriate manner as chairperson you need to have some appreciation of what the appropriateness might be and also be aware of how you are behaving. The chairperson continuum and other models and the described differences between meetings set the scene for guidance. But any approach will be negated if you are so unaware that you cannot recognize what is happening. There is no easy road to this awareness which comes as an amalgamation of various pieces of evidence.

The first requirement is that you develop deliberately an awareness of behaviour and its effects—the effect of your behaviour on others; the effect of others' behaviour on you; and the effect of the behaviour of others on others. This means that you must set out to observe and increase your awareness in these areas. Increased observation by you fits in well with the messages of effective chairpersonship—a chairperson is the controller and maintainer of the meeting, not the principal contributor. The more you are involved in the discussion, the less time and opportunity you have to observe and to control.

It is very difficult to observe or be aware of one's own behaviour. Views can be sought from others whose judgement is valued, but probably the most useful indicator is the effect produced by your behaviour. Do you seem to get into conflict positions frequently? Is it always the fault of the other person? Do people stop listening after you have been talking for a time? Is the reason your manner and method of presentation rather than their inability to listen? Do you find difficulty in eliciting information at an information-seeking meeting? Is your questioning technique suspect; are you taking advantage of various methods rather than be convinced that you can always obtain answers from people who really want to give them? And so on. A useful truism to follow is that behaviour breeds behaviour. People will react to you principally in the same way that they see you approaching them—as they see you, not as you think you are projecting yourself.

Behaviour categorization

The behaviour of people can be categorized and the various categories can be identified as helpful or unhelpful behaviours. Leaders in this approach have been Neil Rackham, Terry Morgan and Peter Honey and they have identified the major general behaviours. These include:

- Proposing
- Supporting
- Defending/attacking
- Open
- Summarizing
- Giving information
- Bringing in
- Building
- Disagreeing
- Blocking/difficulty stating
- Testing understanding
- Seeking information
- Shutting out

These categories can be extended to define the behaviour even further. Other analysts (myself included) have used the categories listed above plus

- Seeking ideas/proposals
- Suggesting (the questioning form of proposing)
- Disagreeing with reasons (the identifiable and more positive form of disagreeing which is retained for bald, unreasoned disagreement)
- Giving views, opinions, feelings (as opposed to simple, factual information)

The categories of behaviour are suitable for use in a number of situations, perhaps with variations to make them more specific or relevant. Concentration can be on specific areas of concern, and on face-to-face, one-to-one interactions. It may be that a group leader is concerned about the ideas and proposals coming from the group when they get together. Concentration can then be on 'proposals' which can be divided into:

- Caught proposals
- Rejected proposals
- Accepted proposals
- Ignored proposals
- Suggestions
- Building, and so on

In the questioning area of your behaviour, behaviour awareness concentration might be on

- Open questions
- Leading questions
- Clarification questions
- Interruptions (suggesting non-listening)
- Closed questions
- Multiple questions
- Probing questions

The category approach offers an objective means of identifying where your principal behaviour falls and may explain why certain aspects are not being as successful as they should be. If you find it too difficult to distance yourself from your behaviour, others can be enrolled in an activity in which they can observe you and record your behaviours in the agreed categories.

Behaviour analysis applied to meetings

One case study research by Rackham and Morgan (1977) was on the behaviour of meeting chairmen. The selection of categories of behaviour was relatively simple and listed

- Content proposals
- Procedural proposals
- Building
- Supporting
- Defending/attacking
- Testing understanding
- Summarizing
- Seeking information
- Giving information
- Bringing-in
- Shutting-out

The next step was considerably more difficult and introduced an area which may be considered as subjective rather than objective. This involved identifying meetings which had effective chairmen, using direct observation and the views of members and senior managers to support the views.

Thirty-one chairmen who satisfied all the criteria were selected and meetings held by these people were observed on at least one occasion using the behaviour analysis categories listed above.

From the behaviour analyses produced a behaviour profile emerged: this is shown in Table 6.1 and the profile of the non-chairmen is also included for chairman/non-chairman comparison.

Table 6.1 Behaviour profiles of meetings

Category	Behaviour by chairmen (%)	Behaviour by others (%)
Content proposals	1.8	11.1
Procedural proposals	9.6	2.4
Building	3.2	2.0
Supporting	5.8	15.5
Disagreeing	2.0	8.4
Defending/attacking	0.1	1.1
Testing understanding	15.2	3.1
Summarizing	11.5	0.7
Seeking information	28.1	16.3
Giving information	21.7	39.4

Source: Rackham and Morgan (1977).

The immediate initial conclusion drawn from comparison of the chairman/non-chairman profiles is the difference of pattern. The analysis would have been very suspect if this had not been so! The comparisons are interesting and demonstrate the types of behaviour which chairpersons should exhibit if they are to be effective.

Both take part in the proposing process, but the structure of each is completely different. Proposals concerned with the running and progress of the meeting—the procedures—come principally from the chair, whereas proposals about the content of the meeting—proposals about the problems to be decided—stem mainly from the members, with a minimal contribution from the chair.

On the other hand, several categories have significant differences: Supporting, Summarizing and Seeking/Giving information. The majority of supporting behaviours come from the members, the chairperson remaining neutral, although having some supporting contributions. Within the neutrality of the chair, these are usually supports for ideas rather than people.

The summarizing profile is predominantly that of the chairperson and rightly so. Some people may be surprised at the relatively high number of summarizing contributions—'My chairperson never summarizes as much as that!' This may be true, but within the facilitator/controller role of the chairperson, summarizing is an important part of the role. Equally important, and demonstrated in the analysis, is the need for the chairperson to check frequently that he or she and the other members have a full understanding of what is being said, proposed and/or agreed.

The two categories of seeking and giving information are almost reversed and reflect the behavioural role of the chair—asking the members for ideas, information, views, then probing for clarification and further information. The members will provide these views, but if they are to be effective they too will ask questions, not only of the chair, but also of their fellow-members, demonstrating an interest in their views. Without this questioning content on the part of the members, the meeting will be seen as a forum for each individual to promote personal views, ignoring those of others—a very ineffective manner of contributing to a meeting. The chairperson will, of course, need to give information—this may be in the early stages of the meeting or each agenda item before turning the process over to the members. He or she will also need from time to time to answer questions from the members.

The effective chairperson

Although the Rackham case study was of a small number of meetings only, and effectiveness was based on almost subjective evidence, the analysis supports a theoretical model based on what you as an effective chairperson should be doing. You should be introducing the subject, then handing the discussion over to the members; you should be controlling the meeting and the members, and keeping them up to date with checks of understanding and interim and final summaries; you should not only be neutral but show neutrality and should be encouraging the members with support for ideas and quests for their views and ideas, either initially or if they are not forthcoming. You will help the members' proposals by building on them from your own experience, but should also be encouraging members to look not only at their own views but also at the views of others, and build on these.

This is the reverse of the all too common profile of the chairperson who dominates the meeting with his or her own views, opinions and proposals; shows little interest in the views of the members and does not encourage them to contribute (but at the end of the meeting complains that they never say anything); and does not help the members to be clear about the conclusions and actions by failing to test understanding and summarize.

It would be satisfying to state that a behaviour modification by the latter type of chairperson to become the former needs only changes of behaviour. In fact this is so, but there is a considerable gap between the intent and the ability to modify in this way. Firstly, there must be awareness of why the, often suspected, ineffectiveness is so. Probably the most effective way of achieving this is for the chairperson to arrange for someone who is skilled in behaviour analysis to attend several meetings and construct profiles.

Motivation to change
If you are considering modifying your behaviour, awareness is not the only factor involved. There must also be a strong motivation to change linked with the assumption that the change will bring about improvements. On a number of occasions I have produced analyses of an individual's behaviour, shown these to him or her and discussed their implications. The response has been 'Yes, I can see that I do these things, and perhaps they are reducing my effectiveness. *But* I am too old to change/I can't see that I can change/I like behaving like that', and so on. The motivation to change, having been made aware of the situation must be self-generated.

One of the advantages of interaction analysis observations is that there is little need for any direction concerning the behaviour profiles produced. If you are aware of the category definitions and the basic structure of behaviour analysis, all that is usually necessary is to see an observation sheet with its record of contributions. Almost every time a discussion will follow about the significance of some of the entries and their implications. This in turn will lead to a discussion about need to change—a discussion in which you must be the leader in deciding what to do.

This self-generation of change motivation will help the third problem, that of actually implementing the change. If you are committed to change, you will seek every opportunity to practise the modified behaviours. Modification, particularly after a lifetime of behaving in certain ways, is not easy and the individual must be encouraged and supported.

If your chairperson behaviour profile shows that reduction in various behaviours is necessary, but that an increase or improvement in other behaviours is also necessary there will be problems. To obtain the reduction in the less desirable behaviours is much easier than increasing the more positive behaviours. To reduce can often mean simply to stop doing or stop doing as much—'I will bite my tongue and not keep interrupting', 'I will not always be the first to speak, and keep on talking', and so on. But to be more active in questioning rather than giving one's own opinion; to restrict proposing and be intent on building; to be more open, and so on, are more difficult to achieve.

Behaviour modification must also be approached carefully in the workplace. The members will react with suspicion if you have always been strong in giving your own views, and you suddenly become a questioner rather than a stater. If there are a number of behaviours to be modified, the changes should be introduced slowly and carefully, otherwise few benefits will accrue.

Your style and approach will have a significant effect on the success and effectiveness of the meeting, but the behaviour of the members must not be ignored. Although it is your own responsibility to ensure that your behaviour is as appropriate as possible, you must also control the behaviour of the members and, as necessary, attempt to educate them in more appropriate behaviours.

Chapter 7

Structuring the meeting

Whatever the type of meeting being considered it will follow a simple overall structure:

- The start of the meeting
- The main part of the meeting
- The end of the meeting
- After the meeting (see Chapter 8)

However, within this basic structure there are a number of variations, principally during the main part of the meeting: these will be considered later in this chapter.

The start of the meeting

You will normally open the meeting, on time, either formally or informally with a few words of welcome. If the meeting is the first of a series commenced for a particular reason, it will be necessary to describe briefly the circumstances in which the series has arisen.

Introductions

In some cases the members may not know each other; you can briefly introduce each member, or preferably invite members to introduce themselves. This introduction should be as brief as effectiveness allows and its content should be governed by the reason for the meeting. A common form of introduction in these cases would be as follows:

- Name.
- Organization and its location if the membership is formed from a number of organizations, parts of a group or simply separate parts of one organization.
- Job title and a brief description if the job is not easily identifiable with the job title.

- Specific interest in the *raison d'être* of the meeting group and any experience in the fields to be covered.

The expenditure of a reasonable amount of time on this process is never wasted because:

- It introduces members in an effective manner.
- It identifies to some extent where expertise and interests lie.
- It ensures that everybody speaks—this can help the quieter members at a later stage of the meeting because they have already spoken and do not need to break their silence at what might be a critical moment.

Obviously there should be no need for this introductory phase if all the members are well acquainted with each other, although an assumption of this acquaintance can be dangerous. If in doubt, ask the members whether they wish to have any form of introduction.

In the case of meetings other than the first of a series, introductions will not be necessary *unless* new members have joined. I stress this point because it is so easy for the chairperson to ignore or fail to recognize the presence of a new member. Consequently that person might sit in the meeting feeling ignored and be very hesitant about making contributions.

Confirmations
The next stage will include confirmation that everybody has received a copy of the agenda and any supporting papers or reports. This will be an opportune time for you to comment if there are any amendments or additions to the agenda, perhaps occasioned by a member requesting meeting time just before the meeting started. It will be necessary to inform the members at what stage the additional item(s) will be considered.

Although the proposed finishing time may have been stated on the notice of the meeting, it is worth while confirming this time at this point in the meeting. The objectives of the meeting may appear obvious from the agenda, but valuable time can often be saved if you state these objectives and offer the opportunity for the members to raise points of clarification.

The main part of the meeting

It is during this part of the meeting that the event becomes effective or ineffective and in addition to being clear about the agenda items, the effective chairperson will have considered in the pre-meeting action how each part of the agenda should be presented and processed. But an open mind must be retained and if the original plan does not appear to be succeeding, or the members are proposing something which has greater advantages, the meeting format must be sufficiently flexible to allow for these variations.

The structure of this part of the meeting will be determined to a major extent by the type of meeting being held and, as suggested earlier, most meetings consist in fact of either different types of approaches or several different types of meeting within one event. In Chapter 2 we saw that meetings or parts of meetings can be described as follows:

- Information giving
- Information seeking
- Consultative or general
- Problem solving and decision making
- Brainstorming
- Team briefing

Most of these types require rather different approaches and, if more than one approach is to be used in one meeting, you must be alert to the need to vary the style of the meeting.

Within these variations there will be variations of style based on the culture of the organization, your preferences and those of the members and the seriousness of the meeting and its objectives. Some meetings are run in a very informal manner with a free and friendly atmosphere. Others, although with an informal atmosphere, are highly structured and follow closely the prepared plan. Yet others are highly formal in their interactive approaches and follow a severely structured format from which little deviation is allowed. There are some situations which, without destroying the openness of an informal environment, still require a reasonably fixed structure.

This structure has the advantage that, for the inexperienced leader, it provides an aid to the leader rather than risk unforeseen developments happening with disastrous consequences. The structure can also help the members to settle down and contribute effectively. Care must be taken, however, not to allow the structure to become so rigid that it destroys the meeting.

Chairperson behaviour

Your behaviour as a chairperson has already been discussed but you
should bear in mind the following:

- The meeting has been called for the members to express their views;
  consequently the contributions of the chairperson must be limited to
  those strictly necessary. If the meeting becomes a chairperson
  monologue, this suggests that the item could have been dealt with in
  another way, for example in writing.
- The principal behaviour of a chairperson is that of facilitator and
  controller of the meeting, seeking the views of the members and
  encouraging them to give these views.
- Frequently, contributions made by members are not as complete or as
  clear as they could have been; another part of the chairperson's role
  is to probe the member for further information or to obtain
  clarification.
- An additional part of the chairperson's role in ensuring
  understanding within the meeting is the giving of interim summaries
  when relevant, and a final summary in every case. These summaries
  will be checked for understanding with the members and any errors
  or omissions rectified.
- The chairperson's role is very much related to the activity of the
  members and he or she will therefore be involved in ensuring that
  contributions are made, that conflict is controlled (not necessarily
  stifled), that there is no dominance by one or more members, and so
  on.

Structures

The descriptions of appropriate structures given here are relevant to
either complete meetings of the type or the parts of a more complex
meeting which will require a number of approaches at different times.

Information-giving meetings

If giving information is the only purpose of the meeting, the structure will
be relatively simple. The meeting process will have the following
structure:

1 A definition and description of the purpose of the meeting, a statement
  of the length of time it will last and a reminder of the terminal
  objectives.
2 A straightforward statement of the information to be given. Care must

be taken in this section of the meeting that an information overload does not take place. If there is a considerable amount of information to be passed, or the information itself is very complex, it should be broken down into digestible/understandable/acceptable bites.

3 At the end of each piece of information the presenter must ensure that it has in fact been heard/understood. There is little value in information if only a section of the audience has either heard it, or if having heard it has not understood it. Consequently the meeting leader must in some way obtain feedback about the reception of the information.

4 This feedback requirement leads to the second major element of an information-giving meeting—seeking information. Depending on the size of the meeting and other factors, the presenter can check out understanding by asking questions of the members. Or you can seek questions of detail or clarification from the members. Or both approaches might be used. But the objective must be that you are completely satisfied that every member has received and understood the information, what is going to happen and what they personally have to do as a result of it.

5 Even though the feedback period appears to show that everyone understands the message by that stage, there is considerable value in consolidating this understanding. The most effective method of doing this is for a summary to be made of the basic points of the information, action points and action roles. Although traditionally this summary would be made by the chairperson, this again puts the members in a passive role. If the meeting environment is suitable, and the member relationships are satisfactory, one or more members can be invited to summarize the meeting, with the chairperson becoming, in effect, a member with the right to challenge any part of the statement. This involvement by the members in the summary will be of considerable value in consolidating their understanding.

Encouraging questioning

Sometimes a group of members might not come forward readily with questions, even though, because of the complexity of the material, there is not likely to be complete understanding. This usually occurs when the group is newly formed and unsure of the other members; although probably all members have a question, they do not wish to give the impression to the other members that they cannot assimilate information. On other occasions, questions of clarification may not be forthcoming when the group is either one of peers or a mixed group across hierarchical levels. Again, the potential questioners do not want to give the impression to their peers, staff or bosses that they have not fully understood.

There are at least two ways of dealing with this situation. If you have the feeling (perhaps as the result of previous experience) that this is likely to happen, before the meeting you can seek the help of one of the members whom you know is not oversensitive about appearing not to understand. This member can ask a question—it does not particularly matter whether it is a personal doubt or not—and once the ice has been broken, there is a greater likelihood that others will follow on.

Where the information is particularly complex, after the information has been given, the group can be divided into small sub-groups, called buzz groups. In these groups they are invited to discuss the information given and formulate questions from the group to be asked when the full group reconvenes. In this way, the originator of the question remains anonymous, but the required information is obtained. Once again it will almost certainly be found that once one or two questions have been asked, inhibitions will disappear and individual questions will start to be posed.

Information-seeking meetings
In this type of meeting or section of a multi-aspect meeting, you will set out to obtain information, views, opinions or feelings about a specific subject. It will usually be even simpler in structure than the type of meeting described above, but its practice might be much more difficult.

1 The starting point will be a statement by you of the desired outcome and the reasons for this enquiry. Such a statement can be concerned with information which will help you or some other individual or group in the organization to make a decision. Or it can be seeking extensive views on a subject so that solution options might be listed prior to the decision-making process. The views, feelings, opinions of the members, either as individuals or as representatives of a wider group, might be sought on an enacted or proposed implementation of a procedure or system. Whatever the nature of the enquiry, it must be made clear why the views are being sought and what will be done with them. It may also be necessary, particularly in the case of sensitive subjects, to define how the comments, etc. will be recorded and how they will be passed on elsewhere, if this is relevant.
2 Seek the information, etc. and probe for clarification, further detail,

wider views, and so on. Maintain the recording agreement made during the first stage.

3 Ensure by some repeat questioning that all the information required has been obtained and if relevant (and it usually is) summarize the information given.

Depending on the relationships within the meeting group and you, it may be necessary to resort to the buzz group tactic in reverse to obtain the information or views. This may be particularly so in the case where views and feelings on organizationally or personally sensitive subjects are sought. You can pose the questions or describe the range of response required, and the group is divided into buzz groups to provide responses. Again, this takes any pressure off individuals by giving them the protection of a group answer. However, you must ensure that it is clear whether the views expressed are those of all the members or whether they are majority views. If this situation is likely or possible, the brief given to the sub-groups will be to report minority views in addition to those of the majority, with an indication of the strength of the minority view. It may then be possible to encourage the minority view holders to comment individually once they see that their views may be swamped if they do not speak up.

Problem-solving/decision-making meetings

This type of meeting is probably the most common type and is exemplified by the usual meeting of members called together to decide on a number of topics listed in an agenda. The simple approach is when there is only one major topic to be discussed and decided upon, but if there are a number of separate items, each can be structured in the same way as one item. Many of these typical meetings, in fact, contain in their agenda not only problem solving/decision making, but items which are information giving, those which are information seeking, and even those which may require a brainstorming approach. It is essential that the appropriate structure is determined for each part of the meeting.

You should take each agenda item in turn, usually as it appears on the agenda, state or restate the objectives or purpose of that item and, if the subject is to be introduced by a member, invite that member to initiate the discussion. In many cases this will be a verbal introduction supporting a paper or report which has been circulated to the members. You should ensure that this presentation is short, clear and impactive and the presenter does not simply read the report out to the meeting.

When the presentation has been completed, in most cases you will then retake control of the ensuing questioning, discussion and decision process (the latter may be simply acceptance of the paper or report, although if this is the case, it may have been more effective to have processed the report other than at a meeting).

You may, perhaps in a coaching role, leaving control of the complete item to the presenter—the presentation, questioning and discussion— although it may be necessary for you to take over for the decision-making process. The meeting will then move on to the next item on the agenda.

A seven-stage decision-making meeting process
Particularly where the member group has convened for the purpose of solving a complex problem and reaching a decision about what has to be done, it will be found useful to follow a seven-stage process. This can also be followed, perhaps with modifications, for each problem-solving/ decision-making item of an agenda.

1 *Informing* Relevant statements can certainly be made at this stage, and some introductory ones will be necessary, but the most effective way of determining understanding and clarity is to ask a range of questions, either of oneself as chairperson, or directly of the members. The questions to ask to ensure that the members are fully in the picture with the meeting requirements will include:
   (i) What are we here for?
   (ii) Is everybody fully aware of and do they understand these objectives?
   (iii) Is everybody clear what is to be done—discuss, review, propose, decide—with the agenda subject?
   (iv) Does the agenda give the necessary information? If not, unclear items should be defined, redefined or clarified.
   (v) How are we going to tackle the subject?
   (vi) Are there any other resources we need to enable this action?
2 *Seeking* Once the subject has been introduced, you will seek from the members the extent of the knowledge held about the subject. Is there any expertise in the subject among the members? What is the range of information held? Has anyone any further information or details? Every attempt should be made by asking questions of a probing and clarifying nature to ensure that all the information held about the subject is brought into the open and everybody has had the opportunity to divulge their knowledge. The final question before

proceeding will be 'Do we have sufficient information with which to proceed, or do we need to adjourn to obtain further information?'

3 *Interim summary* A useful action at this stage, and one which can so easily be forgotten, is to summarize the information held. Particularly if the subject and the information relating to it is complex, recording it on a visible poster is worth while. In complex areas, a paper or report or analytical statement has probably been prepared. Both the preceding stage and the interim summary will still be useful even with this material, because it must not be assumed that everyone will have read the material, or if they have, understood it. Information additional to the prepared paper should certainly be posted so that both sets of information can be used together. But whatever the complete format, you can usefully give a verbal interim summary at this stage before proceeding.

4 *Seeking options* In any problem-solving or decision-making process, the biggest dangers are jumping to conclusions too early; accepting the first solution offered (even if it seems to be the best); accepting that there is only one solution to the problem. Before this happens, you must ensure that all possible solutions are exposed, analysed and discussed, even if some of the possible solutions have already been rejected or do not appear to be suitable solutions. At this stage of the meeting, it may be that a brainstorming session to encourage the emergence of a range of possible solutions might be usefully held. But the assumption must be that there is more than one possible solution to a problem.

5 *Deciding on the most appropriate solution* Among the possible options suggested, there will be some which will be obviously unworkable, some which may require too many extra resources to be operable, some which may be culturally unacceptable, and several which appear to be possible candidates for implementation. This latter group should be discussed thoroughly so that a decision based on total feasibility might be made.

6 *Implementation* Once the solution has been decided upon, the next stage in the discussion must be on the methods, etc., of implementation. How will it be implemented? Who will be responsible for specified aspects of implementation? What other resources are required? Where will the activity take place? When will the (stages of) implementation take place? What are the timetable and deadlines? At what stages will interim reviews take place? Will there be (and when) a final review? And so on until all aspects of the solution implementation have been covered.

7 *Final summary* This will be the final occasion for the actions and

responsibilities to be summarized. The aim should be that on no occasion should members leave the meeting or move on to the next item needing to say to each other 'What exactly is it we are going to do? What was agreed for me to do? When are we going to start?'

Many chairpersons have found it useful to keep a card in front of them during the meeting with the headlines of the stages above noted, to remind them of what they have to do and to ensure that all stages are covered:

1 Inform—what are we here for?
2 Seek information—what do we know?
3 Interim summary—so where are we now?
4 Seek options and discuss—how shall we tackle it?
5 Decide on best solution—is that what we'll do?
6 Implementation—let's take action
7 Final summary—what have we achieved?

And what happens next?

General or consultative meetings
In many ways this type of meeting is very similar to the decision-making meeting except that the process is not carried as far as in that case. These meetings are usually called when the organizer or chairperson needs to discuss, frequently with the team, a subject of common interest; a decision that has been made elsewhere which affects the team and which will eventually have to be implemented; a team or work group process meeting in which the effectiveness and development of the group is discussed. It will be noted that 'discussion' is a word frequently used in relation to this type of meeting, and consequently discussion-leading techniques must be a skill held by the chairperson—this subject will be considered later.

On frequent occasions, although the meeting starts as a consultative, discussion meeting, it becomes necessary for decisions to be made. In such cases you will follow the guidelines suggested above in order to ensure that the situation is approached efficiently.

Brainstorming meetings and team briefings are meetings held for very specific purposes and have formats quite different from the more traditional meeting. These will be discussed later.

The end of the meeting

The closing process will depend on the nature of the meeting that has just been completed. If the meeting has been concerned with one subject for which, for example, problems had to be solved and decisions made, you will complete the meeting with a summary of what has been decided, who is to take what action, how these actions will be undertaken, and during what period of time they will be performed. This should be a brief, clear but comprehensive statement, without extension by reiterating the arguments. In most cases this final summary will have been preceded as the meeting progressed by interim summaries, so there should usually be little need for further questions from the membership. If there are a number of these, you should take this as feedback by the chairperson that queries and doubts were not resolved at the time the particular part of the problem was being discussed.

An alternative approach to this chairperson-controlled summary is to ask the members to provide the summary. This will involve the members in a more active way than passive listening to a provided summary and there is substantial evidence that involvement of this nature ensures greater commitment to the action.

In the case of the more traditional style of 'meeting', that is one with a number of agenda items, each item will have been completed by a summary statement of the decision (if any) and the action agreed. It is useful at the end of the meeting stage for a final summary to be given of the individual agreements reached.

Whichever final summary approach is taken, it should be completed wherever possible within the time limit stated for the meeting, the members thanked for their contributions and the meeting closed.

Summary

Whatever type of meeting is being approached, you should bear in mind that specific actions are required at the beginning of the meeting, during the main part of the meeting and at the end. Additional action is necessary in many cases following the meeting—this will be considered in the next chapter. Guidance has been given on the seven-stage approach, particularly for the problem-solving and decision-making meeting, but this approach has usefulness in other types of event. You should always be aware of your particular role in a meeting which in most cases can be summarized as organizer, convener, facilitator, controller (of structure and behaviour) and summarizer, with your personal contributions limited in most cases to the performance of these tasks.

In addition to remembering the seven stages, chairpersons can usefully remember seven key questions relating to either the whole meeting or individual parts as relevant:

- What are we here for?
- How should we tackle the situation?
- How much do we know already?
- Which decision-making process shall we use?
- What do we need to know, agree, do now?
- What have we achieved?
- What happens next and who does it?

Chapter 8

After the meeting

Basically, the post-meeting action in most cases is to implement what was decided at the meeting. In too many cases there appears to be little acceptance by the chairperson of this responsibility. Of course, there can be little expectation that a chairperson who is not also the immediate line manager of the meeting members who have been given tasks to implement will be required to follow up these decisions. But there should be a mechanism to ensure that they are checked out by someone. The simplest process is delegation at the meeting of tasks and their objectives to members of the meeting who accept responsibility for carrying them out. This requires effective delegation—complete understanding by the delegatee of what is required, parameters of responsibility, time bounds, and so on.

Post-meeting recording

The simplest and least offensive method of advising others of decisions made, and at the same time producing a reminder brief for those requiring to take action, is to produce what can be loosely termed 'minutes'.

Some years ago it would have been unheard of for a meeting to take place and not be recorded by a comprehensive set of minutes, complete to the last detail of who said what. In recent years there has been a move away from this literary achievement to shorter, more impactive, and above all more meaningful documents—the action note.

The action note

The construction of an action note is based on the concept that what happens at the meeting is a process leading to an end result, achievement of the objectives, whatever they might be. As a process the intention is that this should be as efficient and effective as possible, so that when the

meeting is complete everything that needs to be done, has been done—even if this is a decision to adjourn and meet again to continue the process. The meeting itself is therefore process history, an event which has achieved its aims. Consequently the important aspects are now the implementation of the results of this process—action.

This results in the view that the only written consequence of most meetings will be a note which describes solely the action to be taken. 'Most' because some organizations, whether because of legal or procedural requirements, insist on a more traditional form of record—minutes. But unless there are these particular requirements, there seems to be little justification for lengthy records.

Action note structure

To be effective the action note should be short, clear, unambiguous, but sufficiently comprehensive to include everything essential to the implementation of the results of the meeting. It should include an agreed statement of the action decided at the meeting, whether this is in the form of a formal proposal accepted, or a statement of the decision of the meeting. This should be followed by details of the action necessary to implement the agreement:

1 Who is responsible for taking action.
2 If necessary, a detailed description of what is to be done.
3 If necessary, a detailed description of how it is to be done.
4 A statement of the standards to which the action should be performed.
5 Details of timed stages or a final date by which complete action should have been taken.
6 If relevant, where the action is to be implemented.
7 Any authority for the performer to obtain other resources.
8 Details of reviews and action reports deemed necessary, or a statement of responsibility.

These will be the details relating to the agreement which were discussed and agreed at the meeting and which would form the verbal summary by the chairperson. A specimen action note is contained in Figure 8.1.

ACTION NOTE RELATING TO THE MEETING OF THE STAFF APPRAISAL JOINT COMMITTEE HELD ON 31 JANUARY 1992 AT 10.30 a.m.

ACTION NOTE 7/1992

| Present: | Chairperson | Apologies for absence from: |
| | Members | |

DECISION		ACTION AGREED
1 To investigate costs of external printing of report forms		(a) John Smith to produce draft report form for agreement by Report Committee by 15 March.
		(b) Sally Jones to make preliminary investigations of likely costs from three printers, using existing report form. Information to be available by 12 March.
		(c) Fred Cole to discuss Report Forms in use at firms X, Y and Z with their Personnel Managers and make this information available to John Smith by 1 March.
2 Next meeting of this Committee		(a) Date proposed 15 March to receive results of above action and propose further action.
		(b) Chairperson to seek agenda items by 2 March and circulate agenda by 9 March.

Figure 8.1   Part of a specimen action note

If you need them, the arguments for action notes as opposed to minutes include the following:

- Few people read lengthy minutes.
- Required action can be lost in lengthy minutes.
- The essential record is of what is to be done.
- The action note recognizes the contributions of all the members of the team without invidious mention or non-mention of individuals.

The action note format simplifies the process between meetings and at the start of the succeeding meeting. Because it is concerned with action following a meeting, it also acts as a control document with times and dates by which events have to be enacted. At the start of the next meeting, a simple investigation of action taken can be undertaken.

Minutes

Minutes of a meeting are the record of what occurred during the meeting, who was involved and how, what was decided and the steps leading to that decision. Within this framework there can be considerable variation depending on the culture of the organization, the requirements and preferences of the members and the organizations which they represent, and in some cases legal and procedural requirements.

Decisions about the format are relatively simple in the latter cases, construction following the rules of the statutory requirements or the detailed procedures laid down. But even within this apparently straightforward approach considerable variations can occur. The legal or procedural requirement might be, for example, that the proposal, the name of the proposer and seconder, and the result of voting shall be recorded. But custom and practice, and pressure from outside the meeting group might demand that further information is included.

Although superficially the short action note may appear to be the most appropriate form of record, different circumstances may demand something rather different. The question you will need to ask will be 'What is the minimum requirement by you, your members and any other forces in terms of producing a written record of your proceedings?'

Requirements
Whatever the nature of the minutes there are one or two basic requirements which must be satisfied if the records are to be effective.

Accuracy
Firstly they must be true and accurate. If it is necessary to use the contributions of the members in the minutes, the most effective approach is to ensure that the draft minutes are agreed with all concerned before the next meeting when they have to be ratified. It is much easier to resolve a conflict of statement on a one-to-one basis than in open forum.

The use of written notes in whatever 'shorthand' form the writer is capable of are essential if recall is to be complete and accurate. Verbatim notes are unnecessary apart from the times when direct quotations may need to go in the minutes. A useful technique to learn is that of identifying key words and phrases and recording these, either in a traditional manner or as a patterned note form (Buzan, 1974, 1988). Obviously all the notes do not go into the final minutes, but they are an essential set of reference documents, not only when the minutes are being constructed, but at a later date when accuracy may be questioned.

Balanced

This injunction is again one of the problems of recording the contributions and arguments of the members during the meeting. Even though the minute writer may be neutral and impartial, a statement which appears inappropriate or unimportant, but which to the member may be very appropriate and important to the discussion may be omitted. This can certainly result in accusations of partisanship and bias.

This is a difficult situation to resolve, without resorting to the exclusion of all contributions (preferable but perhaps not politic). Again, the clearing of draft minutes by the membership before they are finalized is one way of resolving the problem, but this is not always possible and sometimes undesirable.

Clear

Whatever the form that the minutes might take, as important as their accuracy is clarity. In essence, minutes are working documents which, if full texts, set out to enable members of the group and anyone else who can have recourse to the minutes to understand what the minutes are saying. They are not intended to be literary works of art. The minutes are a factual record which is something to be read and understood away from the meeting and acted upon correctly.

Certainly this demands a correct use of the written language and a basic understanding of syntax and grammatical rules. But it does not require a slavish adherence to the latter if to do so would make the minutes seem ponderous and pedantic and would require much more time to produce. Few people understand, or want to understand, the rules for using 'which' or 'that'; few are concerned about the position of an adverb or the use of a split infinitive, unless the use of these and other grammatical errors cause confusion.

In the absence of other requirements, the words used in the minutes should be simple, avoiding pedantry—for example, 'this point in time' = 'now'; 'I shall give the matter every consideration' = 'I shall think about it', and so on. Keep sentences short. Long sentences tend towards convolution and misunderstanding. But if the document is to be read, it must also flow. Sentences which are abrupt and over-shortened are unnatural for the reader and can become an annoyance. A balance is what is required.

Care must be taken with the use of jargon. Constructed words, acronyms, abbreviations tend to proliferate, but care must be taken in supporting their use. If a long title is in use, write it out fully the first time it is used, thence the recognized abbreviation can be used. In a long text, to avoid loss of the abbreviation's meaning, the full title can be repeated at intervals. Jargon is the shorthand of people who work in a particular discipline. Commonly they use words and abbreviations among themselves which are alien to people outside the discipline. There is no problem in this as long as it is made clear that everybody who will read the minutes will understand the words. This is particularly sensitive when members come from multi-disciplines.

The minute writer must be on the lookout for possible ambiguities. For example, without being pedantic, what does the word 'quite' mean to you? To many people it diminishes the item to which it relates—'he went on a quite long journey' is interpreted as not a short journey, but not excessively long. This is the way in which many British readers would interpret it. But an American reader would interpret 'quite' as 'very'—a completely different emphasis. Look for the specific word, but again without being pedantic, not for the sake of grammatical accuracy, but to ensure unambiguous interpretation.

Brief
It is essential that minutes are as brief as possible. If they become lengthy documents, many of the faults of construction mentioned above are more likely to have crept in. Minutes are intended to be read: long documents face the risk of not being read. Most people when faced with a multi-page document read intently the first side of an A4 sheet; attention starts to wander during the second sheet and after this the remaining sheets receive only a perfunctory glance. This suggests that the document should be preferably one A4 sheet in length, at the most two.

The structure of the formal minute
The actual structure of the minute will depend on the extent to which

contributions are recorded and also on the culture and tradition of the organization.

Minutes, of whatever nature, should always have an identification so that later reference can be made quickly. The title should always include the date and time of the meeting, but to help reference, a number should be given to each set of minutes or action notes. A specimen heading for a set of formal minutes is shown in Figure 8.2. The number of the minutes is at the top left of the page and two options are shown. One is a progressive sequence number relating to the number of times this particular group has met (JPG/10); the other shows the sequence of meetings during a particular year (JPG/1/1992).

JPG/10 or JPG/1/1992

MINUTES OF THE TENTH MEETING OF THE JOINT PERSONNEL GROUP held at 10.30 a.m. on 31 January 1992 in the Board Room, Century House

ATTENDANCE

The names of the members who were present are shown in CAPITAL LETTERS.

Dr A B CEE (Chairperson)	R S Tee
D F GEE	V W EXON
Miss H I JAY	Mrs J S Brown
Ms K L EMM	F W GREEN
N O PEER	Mrs E H SCARLETT
J Black	F R White

Apologies for absence were received from J Black and F R White

Figure 8.2 Specimen head of formal minutes

Each item of the agenda is then recorded in the agreed manner—with full contribution recording, selected contributions or a summarized discussion—and in the order in which it occurred during the meeting, whether or not this was the agenda order. Again, for ease of reference purposes, a number can be accorded to each agenda item. This number can then be linked to the meeting number. The options for this numbering include:

- A sequence 1, 2, 3, etc., for each meeting, giving JPG/1/1992—1
- A sequence commenced at the start of the meeting series—JPG/10—76 or JPG/1/1992—76.

- A sequence commencing at the start of each year. An agenda item for our group at a meeting later in the year could then be JPG/15—76 or JPG/4/1992—20.

Preferences will vary about whether to have the minute number before or after the meeting number—this really does not matter provided everybody involved understands the system and the numbering remains consistent.

A typical format for the minute items is shown in Figure 8.3, the content again depending on the method agreed. Within the minutes reference can be made using an agreed number procedure and sequence with, for example, papers submitted to the group identified by 'Paper' plus 'JPG' (the abbreviations for the group), a sequenced number controlled by the secretary, and the year of the paper—for example, 'Paper JPG/126/1992'.

35. MINUTES OF PREVIOUS MEETING

The minutes of the meeting held on 30 December 1991 (JPG/15/1991) circulated on 5 January 1992 and agreed as a true record were confirmed as such and signed by the chairperson.

36. SECRETARY'S REPORT

The Secretary's report (Paper JPG/85/1991) was accepted following discussion.

37. COST OF PRINTING ANNUAL REPORTS

At the meeting held on 20 November 1991 (JPG/13/1991) V W Exon had been asked to obtain estimates from three printing companies for printing the new annual staff report form (Minute JPG/13/1991—6). He reported the results of these investigations (Paper JPG/80/1991) and it was agreed that a firm quotation should be obtained from Messrs Doitall Ltd for the printing of 10,000 copies of the new annual report for delivery by 30 April 1992. Mr Exon was authorized to take this action and refer the quotation to the next meeting of the Group, when acceptance would be considered.

Figure 8.3 Part of formal minutes specimen

The content of the minutes in this case names the person responsible for the action, gives the information obtained in a summarized and referenced form and summarizes the agreement and action to be taken.

An alternative entry for minute 37 might be:

37. COST OF PRINTING ANNUAL REPORTS

At the meeting held on 20 November 1991 (JPG/13/1991) V W Exon had been asked to obtain estimates from three printing companies for printing the new annual staff report form (Minute JPG/13/1991—6. He described his report (Paper JPG/80/1991) which showed the three estimates obtained. Although the estimate received from Messrs Doless Ltd was the lowest, several members reported that their experiences with this firm had not been good. Some discussion took place about whether this lowest estimate should be accepted, but with restrictive clauses included in the contract. It was finally agreed that the known good record of Messrs Doitall Ltd, the next lowest estimate, should result in them being considered. Mr Exon was asked to obtain a firm quotation from Messrs Doitall Ltd for 10,000 copies of the new annual report form for delivery by 30 April 1992. It was agreed that this quotation would be considered for confirmation at the next meeting.

Timing of minutes

There is only one time to write the minutes—immediately after the meeting or as soon after it as possible. Even notes made during the meeting can turn into vague shorthand expressions after a period of time. 'Immediately' will obviously depend on the time available to the minute writer, but you the chairperson should ensure that this is available. The longer they are delayed the greater the chance of omissions and errors occurring.

Organizational procedure and practice will determine what happens when the draft minutes have been prepared. Normally in the more formal committee situations, the minute writer will send a clean draft to the chairperson who will either confirm or (more commonly) amend the draft and return it to the writer for a clean copy to be produced.

The minutes can then in some cases be sent out, still described as drafts, to the membership who will be invited to comment on or make amendments to the draft. An essential part of this process is to state clearly a final date by which the amended draft must be returned. It should also be made clear that if the draft is not returned by this date, it will be accepted that the member has no amendments. This puts the responsibility where it belongs, rather than keeping the person responsible for writing the minutes in limbo.

A rather more arbitrary approach, although still in use in some organizations, is for the chairperson to be sent the draft minutes for agreement or otherwise. The confirmed minutes are then sent out to the members. This is a very dangerous procedure because the first opportunity which the members have to comment on the accuracy of the minutes is at the start of the next meeting. Unless the meeting approach and the chairperson are then highly autocratic in handling this, a considerable amount of discussion, often heated, can be generated at this stage.

Content of the minutes
At the 'top' end of the range there is the 'Hansard' type of minute, the document produced of the proceedings of the House of Commons. This is a verbatim report, with all contributions entered and attributed to the participating members. There are few other circumstances in which the full text of a meeting is published in this form.

The action note is probably the other extreme of the range as described earlier. Here information is kept to the bare minimum of what was decided and what action has to be taken.

In between these two extremes there are a number of variations, probably best described as a reducing amount of information in descending the range.

Simplified minutes
Where it is not legally or procedurally necessary for direct quotations and full contribution inclusions to be made, the traditional form of minutes can be simplified.

One format of this type excludes the discussion statements by individuals during the consideration of an agenda item. In this case, the discussion is summarized—the introduction, a summary of the arguments for and against and the final conclusion, perhaps in the form of the resolution. Apart from the names of the proposers and seconders, there is no attribution of comments by other members. This simplification is based on the concept that the important outcome of the meeting is the action requirements, in the form of the agreements or resolutions, rather than the process by which these were reached. Otherwise, this format is generally very similar to that of the traditional form.

If you are a new chairperson or taking over an existing meeting series, you should ask the following questions:

- By using the existing form of minutes, are secretarial resources being used in the most effective manner?
- Is there a more effective format for producing a record of the meeting results?
- Are there any legal requirements for the format of the minutes?
- What is the current attitude of the organization to the style of the minutes and how are they likely to react to a variation proposal?
- What kind of records do the members prefer to receive?
- Does the present method of production produce any unwarranted delays both in the clearance of the minutes and at the meetings?

The organization, chairperson or membership has a wide choice with the type of record to be produced for their proceedings. Decisions on the specific format will need to be taken and these will depend on legal, procedural or general requirements and attitudes. Unless there is a specific requirement, not a preference alone, for anything more complex than the simple action note approach, this type of record has much to commend it. It is simple, can be made clear with ease, is short but contains all that members will need to progress the results of the meeting, and runs no risk of offending any member by misquotation or omission of a contribution.

Perhaps one argument offered against the bare record is that there is no record of how a decision was arrived at and this is particularly relevant for members who were unable to attend the meeting. This should be, however, a minor argument which can be rectified easily in a conversation with the chairperson or secretary. The fact that a decision was reached and agreed demonstrates that a process was followed to reach that decision and this decision-making process was an effective one. Perhaps if the decision-making process is suspect, it may be wiser to detail every step in a record! Or more simply, ensure that the decision-making process is effective.

Chapter 9

Controlling the members

Member problem types

We have seen earlier that your task as chairperson is twofold—to control the task so that the objective is achieved effectively, and to be concerned for and responsible for the people who comprise the membership. The latter would present no problems if all members were committed, enthusiastic, interpersonally skilled and able in the performance of meeting requirements. Unfortunately this is rarely so. Consequently you must be able to be aware of people problems as they arise, and be skilled in dealing with them effectively. Some of the members who exhibit dysfunctional behaviour are described below and are:

- The dominator
- The aggressor
- The withdrawer
- The devil's advocate
- The blocker

- The under-contributor
- The comedian
- The recognition seeker
- The digresser
- The side-talker

And in group behaviour

- The over-contributing group
- The moaning group

- The under-contributing group

The dominator

The person exhibiting this behaviour has usually no intention of actively taking over the leadership of the meeting. This is too responsible a position for him or her, so he or she is content to let the chair rest with you, while seeking to dominate within this context, reducing you to a mechanical task processor only.

- Makes contributions so lengthy that others have no time to speak.
- Often contributes in a loud voice, overcoming quieter speakers.
- Always states opinion or information in an over-positive manner.

- If any danger of being controlled is seen, brings in supporters, either previously briefed or from a 'following'.

Control

- Several attempts are usually required as control is not easy.
- Break into the contribution at the earliest opportunity and direct question to another member whom you know has something to say.
- If dominator re-enters the discussion in same way, repeat reference to other's contribution and invite that person to continue.
- Persevere with the re-direction approach in spite of frequent challenges.
- Try not to antagonize the dominator as commonly the contributions from such members can be helpful and valuable if channelled in the appropriate way.
- A direct control approach will usually work for only a short time.

A rather more devious approach can be taken prior to a meeting in which it is anticipated that the dominator will introduce his or her normal behaviour. Ask for dominator's support by keeping quiet 'so that Fred [a normally very quiet member] can be encouraged to speak [and so develop]. You [the dominator] will be playing an important role in helping me [the chairperson] to develop a member and helping that member to become as good a member as you.' An alternative is to give the dominator a specific item which is relevant to the meeting to introduce and control in the anticipation that this will satisfy his or her need to demonstrate dominance to the rest of the members.

The blocker

- Contibutions appear to have little or nothing to do with the meeting.
- Proposals of others are met with disagreement without reasons being stated.
- Constant digressions are raised when the meeting is at a stage of moving on.
- Many people introduce digressions: the mark of the blocker is the number of these introduced and a refusal to keep to the subject.
- Contributions are often made by interrupting others.
- Continues to produce arguments long after it has become apparent that the item has been cleared, and insists on the subject being raised and continued.

Control

- Post-meeting discussion with the blocker to try to determine the reasons for the action—disagreement with other members; need to be recognized, and so on (blocking is rarely done for the sake of blocking without reason, although this does happen).
- If the blocks are disagreements without reasons, insist on reasons being given.
- If the blocks are irrelevant contributions, either thank the contributor and move on or ask for the relevance to the topic under discussion.
- Thank the contributor for the digression and immediately move the meeting on.
- Other approaches will be those used with the dominator.

The recognition seeker

- Member continually draws attention to himself or herself by a large number of contributions and/or lengthy contributions in the belief that this will produce an image of importance.
- Constant reference to the chairperson, usually in a supportive way initially then with the person's own views.
- Frequent interventions are not relevant because speaker has no real knowledge, views or opinions on the subject.

Control

- Again the principal strategy, either on completion of the contribution or, rarely, by interruption, is to turn a question to another member who is likely to speak.
- Other approaches will be the ones used with the dominator.
- Out of meeting action might include having a word with the member prior to the next meeting and saying that although you (the chairperson) know that he or she will have valuable views to offer, you want to develop the other members. So you request him or her to wait until brought in—which you must promise to do, or he or she will come in regardless. Many people react favourably to this form of flattery, in particular the recognition seeker—you are providing recognition but not to the extent that others are ignored, in fact quite the reverse.

The aggressor

This approach is not difficult to recognize, because all contributions are made using aggressive words, tone or manner or a combination of these. The aggression may be directed at you or the other members and can take the form of criticism of a person and his or her views—the more aggressive form of the criticism is when the person is criticized rather than the views. The aggression is often preceded by an interruption of another speaking member and is usually an evident signal of the intention.

Control
This behaviour must be controlled as soon as it occurs. Reactions by the members to the aggression will vary, ranging from the attack being ignored to a full-scale retaliation. If there is obvious retaliation you must take positive action to stop this before it escalates, as escalate it will. If it reaches a conflict level, you have lost control of the now ineffective meeting.

In such cases at the start of an escalation the normal rules that the chairperson should not interrupt members can be reversed. But there is rarely any positive result if you simply step in with an injunction for the two members to cease their conflict—this request/demand is likely to be ignored. Instead

- Cool the atmosphere and give the members in conflict the time to settle somewhat.
- Recognize the conflict but suggest that it is not helping progress and immediately summarize where the meeting has got to.
- Follow the summary with a question directed away from the conflicting members.
- In extreme cases, you must step in, simply stop the conflict and move the meeting on, otherwise the conflict will escalate and destroy both the meeting and your control.

The under-contributor
There is little difficulty in recognizing this member—the member sits during the meeting making either no contributions whatsoever or so very few, in such a non-assertive manner, that they become irrelevant.

Reasons
The reasons are much more difficult to determine, but are very relevant in trying to do something about this dysfunction. There are usually a number of possible reasons why the quiet person may not be

contributing. He or she may know nothing about the subject being discussed and in fact may be at the meeting for one of the wrong reasons. Consequently the member has nothing to say. If this is the case, you must ensure that the attendance is rectified before the next meeting.

In many cases the quiet member is so because he or she is a quiet person who does not like, or finds it difficult, to contribute. This ineffective feeling will be exaggerated if the meeting contains a number of very high contributors who simply do not give the quiet person the opportunity to enter the discussion.

Control
Whatever the reason, it will be impossible to try to determine this until the member speaks. This will be unlikely without assistance. But attempts must be made because once a person speaks the ice is broken and further contributions become easier.

- In most cases, the apparently obvious approach will be to direct a question at the member. This must be done only when you know that the member will have something to say on the subject, otherwise it will make the member withdraw even further.
- Ask another member whom you know has very little knowledge of the subject but is not afraid to admit this. The member will say he or she has little or no knowledge which gives the quiet member the support that he or she is not alone in ignorance. You can then ask the quiet member if there is anything he or she can add.
- Persevere with approaches to the member, even if the initial ones meet with no success.
- If you have no success whatsoever, consider whether the member should be there at all. If the member is there for information only, this can be supplied in many other ways.
- Prior to the meeting, and particularly if the quiet member has specialist or expert knowledge, arrange with the member for him or her to introduce a subject and perhaps lead (with your discreet support) the discussion on the subject.

The danger of the non-contributor is that if others who may not be too keen to speak observe that he or she is being allowed to remain quiet, their contributions may also be lost and an epidemic of non-contribution may result.

The withdrawer

- On occasions a member who normally contributes to the meeting becomes one of the quiet members, even if it is known that he or she has knowledge of the subject.
- A normally contributing member is seen to stop making contributions and physically withdraw from the discussion without the full extent of leaving the meeting.
- Avoidance of contribution is often helped by the member keeping his or her head down so that eye contact cannot be made with you, accompanied by continuous doodling or apparent notetaking.
- In the more active cases of withdrawal, the member approaches the role of blocker by side-talking a lot with the members on each side of him or her, thus interrupting the speaking members and causing the neighbours to miss what is being said elsewhere.

Reasons
On so many occasions the reason for the withdrawal is something you have done or not done—the member has been ignored when he or she wanted to make a contribution; the contribution itself was criticized unjustly, and so on.

Control

- In cases where the withdrawal has been as the result of something you have done, you must apologize in some way and bring the member in.
- If the withdrawal was a reaction to another member, you should have been aware of this and should take action to negate the incident, possibly by referring back to the event and clarifying views or giving the opportunity for the air to be cleared.
- If there seems to be no apparent or identifiable reason for the withdrawal, keep on attempting to bring the member in.
- As a last resort, because reference may exacerbate the member's feelings, you can comment on the withdrawal and ask if anything can be done to resolve the reason. If this path is followed, it is quite normal for the member to deny any withdrawal: in this case, you should continue to bring in the member who will have no excuse for not responding. A different response to your question might be an evasive one; this must not be accepted and you should return with a further probe until a positive reaction results.

The comedian

Another case when recognition is not difficult. Many meetings contain the group comedian who at every opportunity instead of making a worthwhile contribution comes out with a joke, quip or humorous remark. On many occasions this can be a valuable contribution: when there is a danger of a conflict starting; the atmosphere has become strained for some reason; members are starting to feel strain or tiredness, and so on. But an excess of this behaviour starts to interfere with what is after all the serious business of the meeting. It is too easy for the perpetual joker to become a bore, a nuisance and a time waster.

Control

You must be aware when the humour has gone beyond an acceptable level and there is a danger that it can disrupt the meeting.

- The humorous contribution can be acknowledged as such, but you can then ask if he or she has anything relevant to contribute. If this happens once or twice it has to be an obstinate comedian who does not accept the message.
- The repeated attempts at humour can be simply ignored. Frequently the members themselves either do this or tell the comedian to shut up.
- If none of these methods is effective, you must take a stand and ask the comedian to make a serious contribution to the meeting.
- If the comedy is the member's only contribution, although this is rare, you should consider whether the member should be included in the meeting in the future.

The digresser

- Digressions or red herrings are usually subjects raised which have no relationship to the subject under discussion, often a member recounting an experience of some personal nature or describing something about which he or she has heard.
- It is used frequently by the blocker, but also a naturally occurring behaviour of some members who often like the sound of their own voices or are unaware that they are interrupting the meeting with what they think is a relevant or valuable anecdote whereas it is usually neither of these.
- The digresser is often also long-winded and ignores interruptions, even by the chairperson!

Control

Often all that can be done, and something must be done if this becomes
a repetitious occurrence, is to allow the speaker to reach the end of the
story, then intervene. The intervention, so as not to upset the speaker who
may otherwise be a useful member, can comment on the importance of
what has been said. Then a question can be directed at another member,
or the speaker might be asked if he or she has anything to say
specifically related to the subject. You must be prepared to do this on
more than one occasion, as one attempt may not be sufficient to make
the speaker realize what he or she is doing.

The devil's advocate

This member is the one who can be relied on to say 'Yes, but let's look at
the other side of the problem . . .'. So often this is a valuable assistance to
the members who may have locked-in on one approach which may not
be the most appropriate. The devil's advocate wakens others to other
possible solutions, views, opinions, and so on. If this approach is used at
the times when it is appropriate, it is a valuable behaviour. But there are
people who always take the other point of view, whether or not it is
appropriate or realistic to do so. These types become a nuisance and
delayers of the decision-making process.

Control

If you become aware that the advocacy is being introduced in the latter
way and for recognition-seeking reasons, a strong line should be taken
and the contribution stopped in ways suggested for the recognition
seeker, blocker or dominant member.

The side-talker

One of the most disruptive influences in a meeting is when one member
continually talks, either in an audible whisper or in normal tones, to
neighbouring members. Frequent side-talk of this nature

- interferes with the continuity of the discussion,
- disturbs the listening by yourself and other members,
- if it is unwanted by the member(s) approached, stops them hearing
  what is being said elsewhere.

Side-talking by more than one pair of members usually indicates that
something is going wrong with the meeting: the discussion has become

irrelevant; issues exist but are not being raised; or a variety of possible causes.

Control

- If it is only one pair of members, stop the discussion and ask if the members have some relevant point to make about the subject as the rest of the members did not hear what they were saying (it may be necessary to do this on one or more occasions before the side-talk ceases).
- If there is wider side-talking occurring, raise the question that there seem to be issues not being cleared and request the members to raise them. If there are serious issues, these will almost certainly be raised. If nothing is raised, the likelihood is that the subject is being drawn out unnecessarily—confirm that all has been said, and move on to the next topic.

Summary

The member types described above do not represent all the possible dysfunctional behaviours, but they are the most significant ones and others are usually variations on the theme.

In summary, you will have three basic approaches possible, one of which is never to ignore the behaviour if it becomes repetitive. The behaviour can be confronted, in the most effective way possible, at the end of the contribution. The discussion can be directed away from the dysfunctional member to other members. Or following direction away from this member to other members, the behaviour can be confronted after the meeting to resolve any problems that may be causing it.

A final approach, which must be used with care but which must be used if necessary, is simply to tell the dysfunctional member to desist as it is upsetting the rest of the members. Use of this approach will normally depend on the group, the relationships with the chairperson and within the group, and the atmosphere which normally prevails in the group. However, even in the best of these cases, to tell Fred to 'Shut up' may work on 99 out of 100 occasions, but on the 100th Fred may feel that this is unjust, that people have not recognized the value of what he was saying, and he may react in a way that is not his norm.

Group behaviour

Group over-contribution

The complete membership group can become a problem through either over- or under-contribution. Over-contribution can make the meeting ineffective and is often due to enthusiasm for the task. Everybody has a contribution or a proposal to make and is intent on making it, with the result that nobody is listening to anyone else and perhaps the only proposal that is accepted is by the member with the loudest voice or the most persistent approach.

Consequently it is possible that good proposals are missed or rejected without realistic discussion. At the end of a meeting of this nature there are usually some members satisfied because their proposals went through, but a number of others very dissatisfied because of their failure to have their proposals even listened to.

Your objective in such a case must be to slow the discussion down sufficiently to enable proposals to be taken account of. In most cases within a group each individual who has an idea or proposal is principally interested in that idea only and is waiting for the opportunity to present this idea. Consequently the ideas of others are not really listened to and certainly not given the consideration they deserve.

One effective method of controlling this natural exuberance is to ensure that all proposals are given full consideration. Instead of permitting the initial proposal of 'What I propose is . . .' to be followed by another member saying 'Yes, that's all very well, but I suggest we do . . .', the discussion is controlled from the initial proposal. No counter-proposal is permitted after the initial proposal. Instead, you might ask 'This is what is proposed? What do you see as the good points and the poor points of it? Can anyone suggest a way in which it can be improved?' This approach encourages the other members, rather than concentrate on their own ideas, to consider this first proposal and if possible build upon it. Each proposal is dealt with in this way in turn, thus ensuring that every proposal is considered sufficiently. Frequently this reduces the number of proposals because many similar proposals may be amalgamated, making the original proposal a much more substantive proposal than when it originated.

This approach, which supports building above any other initiative behaviour, is the opposite approach to brainstorming which seeks to introduce as many ideas as possible without discussion of them.

Group under-contribution

The approach to the under-contributing group has to take a completely different path. In this case we have a quiet group compared with only one or two quiet members. The reasons for this can be many and can include epidemic infection by one or two members; disinterest in the task; non-cooperation with the chairperson; climatic variations, etc. Let us assume that the membership is not against the leader or the task, but that a number of other factors have combined to make them less than effective and articulate. Exhortation by the chairperson is not likely to produce any dramatic change as a meeting gives many opportunities for a passive approach.

Your intention should be to obtain views, proposals, solutions, etc., and consequently you have to motivate or move the members in some way to achieve this. One usually successful approach which has been mentioned earlier is to divide the group into smaller, buzz groups. The buzz groups are either given separate, specific tasks to do—to provide x solutions to the problem; to collect and summarize all the individual views; to look for the advantages and disadvantages of a particular approach. In smaller groups the members are more likely to participate than in the full group where there is a greater opportunity to hide, and the results can have a greater degree of risk, being effectively anonymous. Each group can be asked to report and, as by this time the activity level is usually higher, the full meeting can be given the task of collating the results.

The moaning group

Sometimes, when the organization is in a state of change which the members either do not understand or have feelings strongly against, meetings, of whatever nature, can degenerate into moan events. Whatever you try to do, even perhaps threatening sanctions, the members are not interested in the subject of the meeting, only with relieving their own feelings. In such cases, you have two principal options. One, a draconian measure, is to close the meeting. This unfortunately does not solve the problem, it only suspends it until another occasion when again it will have to be dealt with.

One alternative, which has been used on a number of occasions with success, is not only to allow the moans, but to encourage them. This has to be done, however, on a horsetrading basis. For example, when the situation has reached such a stage that continuing normally would be useless, you can propose 10 minutes during which the members can express their complaints. But, in return, after this period, a further period should be allotted so that the members can propose positive ways in which their complaints might be resolved. This approach has the benefit of turning a negative situation into a positive one, utilizing the skill and experience of the members in a way that is clearly seen by them. You must, of course, agree to take note of the complaints and the proposed solutions for consideration by either yourself or others.

Once these matters have been resolved, the meeting can return to its normal business, the secondary agenda having been cleared as an obstruction to progress.

Chapter 10

Discussion leading

Apart from meetings in which the boss stands up, makes a statement to the assembly and then retires without questions or discussion, discussion is the principal activity of a meeting. General or consultative meetings particularly will be run along fully discussive lines. Within other meetings, as soon as the chairperson offers the subject to the members for discussion, the same discussion objective is involved. This process is known as the discussion-leading technique, the principles of which apply equally to specific discussion meetings and sections of a complex agenda meeting.

The role of the discussion leader

The discussion leader takes what appears to be a very passive role as, normally, having introduced the subject, the members are left to decide their methods and to work their own ways through and out of problem situations. Although your role will appear to be a passive one, instead of contributing to a significant extent you will be very active in listening and absorbing what is said. There can be occasions when at your suggestion or at the request of the members, you might become a fully integrated and participative member of the discussion group. This can cause problems, one of which might be that you will be given a hearing on the basis of your senior position, rather than the weight of what you have to say. Also, of course, the more involved you might be in the discussion, the less opportunity there will be to practise control and support activities.

Preparation

The content and extent of your preparation to lead a discussion group are very similar to those of the chairperson of a 'conventional' meeting.

Objectives

Your objectives and those of the discussion meeting will depend on the subject of the meeting, but will normally include the following:

- What end result is required for this meeting?
- What do I want the members to have learned by the end of the meeting?
- What other knowledge do I want the members to take away with them by the end of the meeting?
- What do I hope to learn as a result of the discussion?
- (If the discussion is part of a more complex meeting) How does this discussion relate to the overall meeting objectives?

The topic

A number of questions will need to be asked concerning the topic for discussion.

- What knowledge and experience have the members of this topic?
- What is the level of knowledge and experience held?
- If this is not known, what action can be taken to determine it?
- What is the likely level of interest in the topic?
- Bearing in mind the membership content, how controversial is the subject likely to be?
- Are there any aspects of the topic that may offend any of the members?

The existing knowledge and experience aspects are important in determining the level at which the discussion and also your involvement should be pitched. If the subject is new to the members, initial discussion will have to be at a relatively elementary level with you feeding an amount of information to the members to support their discussion. You must be careful in these circumstances not to assume too little knowledge on the part of the members and take on the role of information giver to too great an extent.

If, however, the topic is one which is known to the members, the discussion will probably be concerned with specialized, detailed or developmental aspects. In this case you can take a very low profile role and give the members full rein in the discussion.

Analysing a topic

In the more formal types of discussions, usually when there is some knowledge but little expertise—a common level in discussions—you will need to analyse the topic before the discussion to ensure that as much as possible is gained from it.

Shopping list plan
A detailed analysis can produce a valuable tool for you to refer to during the discussion. This is basically a shopping list of the aspects of the topic which should enter into the discussion. You can prepare this by using the horizontal planning approach used by presenters.

A sheet of paper, usually best laid out horizontally rather than vertically, is used as the base for building ideas. Along the top of the sheet, not necessarily in a logical order, should be entered the key points or ideas relating to the topic. For example, if the meeting is to discuss the introduction of management training into the organization, some of the headings could be:

- Level
- Range
- Training/development
- Internal/external
- Residential
- Cost
- Evaluation

You would then consider each heading, not necessarily in turn, before moving on to another, and write under each heading a list, as complete as possible, of aspects relating to that heading. In the example above, the entries under the first heading might include:

- Level
    - Senior, middle or junior
    - All or some
    - General and/or technical
    - Head office and/or field locations
    - Mixed or level groups
    - New entrants and/or experienced managers
    - Volunteers or compulsory
    - How need decided

Pros and cons list

An alternative to the straightforward shopping list is to produce a prompt list of pros and cons or advantages and disadvantages when this is appropriate to the type of subject.

Divide a sheet of paper vertically with headings 'Pro' on one side and 'Con' on the other. The discussion leader will then consider as many advantages and disadvantages relating to the topic as possible and list these in the relevant column. If a subject such as the management training example quoted above is being discussed, a subject in which there will be a number of key areas, the list can be divided with headings of this nature. So the prompt list will start with 'Level', under which will be listed the pros and cons relating to the aspects of this key area: mixing management levels; mixing general and technical managers; mixing head office and field managers, and so on.

Similar lists would be produced for each of the headings until the analysis represented a complete shorthand list of as many aspects relating to the topic that the discussion leader could think of. The list could then be re-formed with the headings in a logical order to discuss, and the sub-headings analysed for completeness.

In addition to acting as a meeting prompt for you, it may also act as a trigger to obtain additional information before the meeting.

During the discussion

Introducing the topic

This will require a clear definition or perhaps redefinition of a declared subject followed by guidance about the discussion, its purpose and parameters.

Some discussion leaders feel that by starting the 'discussion' themselves with a statement of information or how they see the topic will then encourage the members to start contributing. It may, but there is also the danger that when the members hear you making an extensive contribution, they may become passive and the start-up problem remains when you stop talking.

In the majority of cases, a planned introduction by you will help the transition from the opening to encouraging the members to enter the discussion. Usually once they have started, unless you keep intervening, the discussion will gather momentum.

The topic for discussion can be written on a sheet of flipchart paper and displayed in front of the discussion group so that it is always there as a reminder of what is to be discussed. You can then introduce the topic verbally. The objective at this stage is to introduce the topic in such a way as to make it sound interesting and worth while to discuss. Following the opening statements you can make what can be considered as an opening contribution. This will relate to the topic and should be linked to the first, important key area on the 'shopping list'. Any background information concerning the topic should be given in as brief a form as possible. In the management training example given above, the statement could be to the effect 'that the organization is considering introducing management training on a more organized basis and would appreciate the views of the group on as many aspects relating to this as possible. The views of the group would be recorded and passed to senior management who would decide on the next steps—decision, reference to a decision group, cancellation, etc.'

Starting the discussion

The next step is often best expressed as a question to the group, and as suggested above this should relate to the first trigger item on the key area list. On occasions a 'shock tactic' of asking a question before defining the subject to be discussed can produce a suitable reaction. An example of this might be:

1 On a sheet of flipchart paper write boldly '2 out of 3'.
2 Ask the members what that statement means to them. A number of possible interpretations result.
3 When the interpretations have been exhausted, possibly without your intent emerging, write the word 'marriages' underneath the first entry and ask if this helps. Depending on the group this may give the intent away.
4 If the full statement does not emerge write 'end in divorce' below the last entry.
5 Quote the most recent, reliable statistics on the rate of divorce and suggest that the group discuss this problem and consider what might be done to change the situation.

This could be a 'different' starter for a discussion on divorce. Otherwise the opening question might be in a more traditional manner.

Maintaining the discussion

Once the discussion is under way, your role is to ensure the continuity of this discussion, help the members to cover as many as possible of the aspects of the topic and, if relevant, to come to some conclusions.

During the discussion you can refer to the shopping list or pros/cons prompt and as aspects are discussed to the necessary extent, the item can be marked off until all the items required to be discussed have been eliminated.

Otherwise you act as a helpful controller of the discussion and of the people, reacting to the various types of member in the most appropriate way and offering information if the members appear to have this need. If not, you should intervene only when circumstances demand that this is the only action relevant.

Probably one of your more difficult tasks will be to sit and listen to the group going down an ineffective road; the natural reaction is to intervene and redirect it to the 'correct' path. Initially you should not intervene but leave the group to discover its own way out of the problem that it created itself. However, if it appears that non-intervention will destroy the discussion objectives, or there is a severe time limitation which does not allow unlimited time for the group to develop its own destiny, you must decide on some action. This will preferably be not to tell the group what to do but rather to draw its attention to the problem and suggest that corrective action be taken.

Silent members
As part of your people control the type of person you should be watching for more than others is the silent person. An intervention here is warranted because the rest of the group may not notice this withdrawal. It must not be assumed that silent members are not interested, nor that they are not learning something, but until they say something even this will not be known.

The expert
The 'expert' must also be controlled, otherwise the discussion may degenerate into a monologue with the other members neither contributing nor learning. By all means use the member's expertise, but usually as a means to generate questions and resultant discussion among the other members.

Questioning

Your contributions will certainly weigh heavily towards questioning, usually to help understanding among the members. While you are listening actively, you may hear comments which are not picked up by the other members—usually because they are so involved in what they want to say that listening is not a high priority. A member may make a very general comment without supporting the statement; an incomplete contribution may be made because the speaker may either simply fade away or be interrupted; a controversial statement which deserves a challenge might not be heard or challenged. These are situations in which you should intervene with a question, effectively bringing the group's notice to the missed contribution. Usually the type of question will be of the open variety or an invitation to do something.

Typical leader questions can include:

'John, you seemed to suggest when you spoke that . . . What experiences have you had that make you think so?'

'What makes you think that?'

'Would you please give an example to illustrate that point?'

'Mary said earlier that . . . I'm not sure everybody heard what she said. Would you say it again Mary as I think it could be an important point?'

Ending the discussion

It is at the end of the discussion that you have a positive and overt role to play. Whatever interventionist or participative role you have taken during the discussion, the final summary is your 'responsibility'. This responsibility does not necessarily mean that it will be you who gives the summary. If the group has been responsible for the discussion, it is more appropriate for the group or one of its members to produce the summary. Your role is then one of ensuring that this summary is comprehensive, accurate and complete—as it would have been if you had been giving the summary yourself.

It can help comprehensiveness, correctness, comprehension and retention if whoever is giving the summary writes up an abbreviated version as it is being given verbally. This approach can be helped if interim agreements and conclusions are written up during the discussion as a continuous process so that the final summary is a reprise of the listed single summaries.

Chapter 11

Team briefing and brainstorming meetings

Team briefing

Team briefing is a systematic process rather than a singular meeting technique which includes meetings of people, but in a more specific manner than in 'meetings' generally.

Many organizations hold worker or staff meetings; some of these are frequent, others are held at very infrequent intervals; some are good meetings which are member-centred and oriented, others are unhelpful, unwanted, over-formal, leader-centred; some are short and impactive, others extended, boring and hinder the work process rather than help. And, of course, many others fall between these extremes.

Team briefing is an attempt to produce an effective form of communication within an organization, effective in that it produces the maximum effect within the minimum amount of resource time. It is also communication practised in the smallest practical and practicable units— a production section, or even parts of that section, depending on the discrete nature of each group. It tries to rectify the effects that management neglect of effective communication has produced and involve the total workforce in the communication of facts, decisions, problems and the reasons for them.

Benefits

The benefits should be that there is increased commitment both to work and the communication process, not only among the shop floor workers (this is usually where an increase of commitment is aimed), but throughout the hierarchy to top management level. Workers on the shop floor frequently complain that nobody takes any notice of them; managers at the top complain that nobody tells them anything and often no notice is taken of what they want; and people in between complain of both these aspects plus the complaint of always being ignored/criticized from above and below.

Another benefit should be that misunderstandings are reduced. The team briefing process, because of its controlled approach, ensures that the right people hear what they should be aware of and have the opportunity to clarify any non- or misunderstandings.

A third benefit is that the potentially damaging effects of the grapevine communication method are reduced by ensuring that it is not necessary. In team briefing members are kept up to date with changes, problems, situations so that damaging (usually to management) rumours do not circulate. If the workforce has heard about something through the grapevine, and this rumour is incorrect, it becomes much more difficult at a subsequent meeting to convince the workers of the true message. It is an unfortunate fact that if people are not told early about what is happening or going to happen, they will believe the information they receive in other ways.

Finally, a benefit of effective team briefing should be an increase in the ability of the workforce to cooperate with and achieve change. If people are aware as fully as possible of what is happening, what is required of them, what others are doing and why, the likelihood of acceptance of the change is increased considerably. On too many occasions conflicts, disagreements, strikes, walkouts and other negative forms of action have taken place because of misunderstanding of the reason for change— usually because it was not explained.

The structure of team briefing

The concept of team briefing and team briefing groups is simple and follows some equally simple principles:

- Briefing is by face-to-face communication.
- Briefing groups are kept to a reasonable size.
- Briefing meetings are held at regular intervals.
- The briefing at a meeting is relevant.
- Understanding is checked.
- Support for the briefing groups exists throughout the organization,

Face to face

The problems of attempting to communicate by means other than verbal, face to face with people, have been discussed earlier, and there is no doubt that the face-to-face approach whenever it is possible is the most effective. The language, content, method of presentation can all be controlled so that they are appropriate for the group involved, and there is the opportunity for the leader to check understanding and for the members to raise points of confusion.

The restriction in size for team briefing, as we shall see later, means that many of the formal arrangements for meetings are not necessary and ideally the team briefings can be held in the workplace—the shop floor, the accounts office, the sales support office, and so on.

One of the aspects of team briefing meetings is that they are kept as short as possible, and because they contain aspects in which the members are interested, there is often little need for the members even to be seated. However, a number of factors must be considered before this informal approach is used—visibility of people and charts, disabled members, and so on. The workplace may not be suitable although preferable. This area may be part of a larger area where others are working with consequent noise and other distractions. But the choice of an alternative meeting place should avoid over-formal surroundings which might inhibit communication—there are often canteens or rest rooms available which might be suitable.

Honesty

An essential element of the team briefing is honesty. If you have information and can disclose this, do so; if you are asked a question and do not know the answer, admit this but undertake to find out the answer and let everybody know; if there is some further information that you are not allowed to disclose, say so and undertake to inform participants as soon as you are allowed to do so.

Timing

The timing is often an important element. The end of the day is not an effective time, nor often is first thing in the day. Shiftworking can present problems. Ask the people concerned how they want to tackle this possible problem. It may be that the team briefing can be held at the overlap of two shifts, the outgoing shiftworkers receiving overtime for their staying, and the incoming workers using this early part of the shift for their attendance. It may be necessary in a continuous working process to make some cover arrangements for the duration of the short briefing meeting.

However, shiftworking may cause no problems, particularly if the briefings are looked on as team approaches. Within one shift there will be a number of teams who can have their team meetings within the shift;

the next shift has its own team who will hold their own briefing meetings. As long as everybody is being treated equally and receiving the same messages, this works well. Problems occur, not only with shifts but with numbers of teams, if some teams are treated well and receive all information, whereas other teams have restricted activity and information.

Reasonable size

It is difficult to lay down guidelines about this as circumstances will vary from one team to another, from one department to another and from one organization to another. The most effective size for a team briefing meeting is between four and twelve people, although the upper figure can be extended slightly if necessary. The ultimate guide must be the membership of the team rather than a model size limitation. But if the size becomes too large, you may question whether the group is one team only or more than one team can be identified. In this case the teams are separated, and relevant, smaller team briefings held.

The size of a group can have a number of effects. The principal one is that discussion is easier and more relevant in a smaller, homogenous group rather than a large group made up of people from dissimilar teams. What the discrete group is discussing relates to the members and they can identify easily with this. In the larger meeting, much of the content will either not relate to them or they are unable to make a connection with their own work.

Regular intervals

One of the problems of meetings held other than on the team briefing basis is that because large meetings take a large proportion of resource time and are not often seen as effective, they are held at intervals, which if the chairperson and/or members can effect it, become longer until the meetings cease to be held or become annual jamborees.

The essence of team briefing meetings is that because they are kept short, they can be held at regular and frequent intervals. Weekly, fortnightly or monthly meetings are possibilities, but certainly not longer than monthly as they may then cease to have an impact. However, if there is nothing to pass on, and it is known that there is no business to come from the team, do not hold a meeting just for the sake of it.

Once the pattern of team briefing meetings is established, members usually enjoy them. One useful approach is to hold initially weekly meetings of short duration then, when the concept of team briefing meetings is established, part of one meeting might be a discussion on the required frequency of meetings.

The timing of the meetings may need to be considered in relation to other team meetings held which have a bearing on the group—for example, the meeting of the senior management team will supply information for discussion by the teams lower in the hierarchy, so these might usefully be held closely following the senior management meeting.

Relevant
What should be included in a team briefing meeting? The response to this question could be very wide, but the answer must hinge on relevancy. The material must be relevant to the team concerned. It may be very pleasant hearing about a lot of things which do not concern the group but are 'interesting', but these items take up valuable time and reduce the time available for relevant items. Relevance must also be considered in the context of whether the item should be brought up at a meeting, or would be more effectively processed by some other means. Experience of many organizations holding briefing meetings has shown that the following should be borne in mind for inclusion.

1 *Progress* This is informing the team how well or badly it is doing as a team, relating this to such factors as the effect on other teams and the organization, in addition perhaps to the effect on such things as the bonus. But the detailed (and boring/unclear) analysis of items not of relevance to the team should be avoided or mentioned only briefly.
2 *Personal* Information that will affect the team members as people will be relevant, but not personalized or individual comments—these should be kept for private counselling sessions. Items that might be included are team changes; important changes in the organization which will have an effect on the team; news of changes in pay and conditions; lateness and absenteeism which is having an effect on the team results (otherwise it is not relevant and again should not be personalized).
3 *Senior management briefing* When you are producing your agenda for the meeting, it will be necessary to obtain from the senior management team a briefing on what it wants to be passed through the organization. Commonly this results from initially the senior management team meeting which discusses its agenda and agrees a briefing statement on matters of, for example, policy changes about which the organization

should be told; procedural and system changes; legal effects. Following this senior meeting, the team briefing at the next level will be held, usually led by the managers who are individuals on the senior team. Each will hold a team meeting with his or her immediate team and, in addition to matters relating directly to that team, the senior brief will be passed on. The managers forming that team will have teams of their own. From the senior brief they have received they will extract relevant parts for their meetings (some may only need to go to certain levels or departments). And so on down the briefing line.

This approach is quite different from the mushroom approach when senior management issues a brief which everybody must receive, whether it is relevant or not and which can be distorted in its movement down the organization. You, as team leader, should consider what information you have received should be passed on.

The process also works in the opposite direction. In addition to being given information at the briefing meeting, the members will bring up and discuss items from their points of view. If it is relevant to do so, you will take these items to the team meeting of which you are a member, and so on up the line to the relevant highest level.

Checking understanding

An essential element of communication is the checking and monitoring of the understanding of the communication in whichever direction it is moving. The controlled size of team briefing groups helps this process to a very large extent. In large meetings, even if an attempt is made to check whether a communication has been received, there are always people who have not understood but, because they do not want to lose face in the large company, do not disclose their non-understanding. In the smaller briefing groups, more 'face' is lost by not saying that something is not understood or seeking clarification, then going away and making errors for all to see. Until the team has developed to the extent that its checking is self-generating, you must frequently ensure that everything has been understood by everybody.

Full organizational support

It is simple to hold meetings of the traditional kind on various level bases, each meeting being more or less independent of any other meetings that might be held. But team briefing meetings, because of the octopus-like chain connections must have the support of everybody in the organization. This must be particularly so in respect of the higher levels of management. If team briefing groups are to succeed at the 'shop floor', supervisory and junior management levels, they must be seen to be in evidence and succeeding at the higher levels. Consequently, team briefing cannot be simply installed in an organization without positive and active commitment being obtained for it at all these levels, starting with a visible and positive statement of support by senior management.

Briefing groups should not be initiated with the first meeting being one of nothing but bad news—reduced bonus, redundancies, pay cuts—or even the announcement of a major change. If these items form the basis of the first meeting, any subsequent meetings will be looked upon with suspicion as the harbingers of bad news. It is desirable, although not always possible, for the first meeting to be one of good news, although even this may set up expectations which may not be fulfilled.

Preparation for team briefing

Your preparation for team briefing meetings should be similar to that for traditional meetings. It is a useful plan to diary team meetings in conjunction with those of the next line above, so that the brief which is being passed on can be received and considered. This brief can then be considered with the local briefing material to be raised and whether the essential brief passed down means that there will not be time for some of the local items.

Once the pattern of meetings has been established, a simple confirmatory notice only will be necessary, but a rather fuller notice in sufficient time should be issued.

A simple although rarely considered practice can often be helpful in creating and/or maintaining an open attitude within the team to the briefing meetings. The normal practice for chairpersons of meetings is to maintain a file with material concerning the meeting, and apart from issuing minutes or action notes, retaining this file. It is worth considering making this an open file by having the information filed in an area easily available to the team so that members can see everything that is happening in connection with their meeting.

Brainstorming meetings

Brainstorming is a particular technique for the production of ideas in a creative manner, and consequently lends itself easily to the meeting process. A brainstorming meeting is quite different from the normal type of meeting and requires specific techniques and attitudes.

Creative thinking

The basis of brainstorming is in lateral or creative thinking. Problem solving usually takes the form of a logical analysis of the problem to be approached, the logical path following the steps of identifying the problem; describing the problem environment; seeking possible solutions; deciding which solution will be the most effective; and implementing the decision. Brainstorming enters this logical path at the possible solution generation stage, although there must be some separation from this logical approach.

Logic will permit the decision makers to progress through most of the steps described above, but the very constraints of logic can inhibit the possible solution generation process. Logic demands a close attention to detail, to precedents, to the most effective ways possible. This is a narrow path in many cases. Original, novel, even more effective solutions may not be generated by this process, but it is here that brainstorming with its much wider thinking approach might help.

Many barriers to creative thinking exist within us, some imposed by our education, others by what we read and hear. The barriers of conformity, logic, apparent bounding, convention, history and often the fear of making a fool of ourselves restrict our creative thinking. The 'bouncing bomb' would not have been invented during the Second World War if creative thought had not been brought to the apparently impossible task of breaching the German dams.

It is the application of this approach to thinking that enables the practice of brainstorming.

Brainstorming

It must be made clear that the practice of brainstorming is not to make decisions but simply to generate as many possible solutions or ideas as possible. From this generated list, the most effective solution can be selected.

Although the purpose of the brainstorming is to encourage creative thinking, an anomaly exists in the actual running of a brainstorming meeting. It would be anticipated that because creative or freewheeling thinking is to be used, the structure and discipline of a formal meeting would be ignored. In fact a brainstorming meeting is held under the strictest of structural and controlling disciplines.

The reason for this disciplined approach, which eschews discussion of the ideas generated, is that with comment or discussion, barriers to free thought might be easily erected. Members of a brainstorming meeting are encouraged to think not only widely, but perhaps also wildly. This may, in normal circumstances, evoke ridicule of the person and ideas.

It is therefore important that during the brainstorming meeting, any idea or suggestion is received without discussion, comment and certainly not scorn.

Non-discussion has another benefit. If, after every suggestion a discussion is held, the flow of ideas is seriously interrupted and barriers are erected by the length of the discussion itself. A mind that has to switch on and off to logical thought and discussion is less likely to provide a flow of creative ideas.

The role of the chairperson

In a brainstorming meeting you have a completely different role from that in a more traditional type of meeting. The agenda is simple—a statement of the problem to be approached and the generation of suggestions, ideas and proposals. You have a controlling role, but very different from the traditional one. In a brainstorming meeting your almost sole function is to encourage members to come up with a flow of ideas. This will be encouraged by your stopping any discussion or comment on ideas produced by members. This control is dictatorial; as soon as any discussion starts you must put an end to it, even to the extent of stating boldly and bluntly 'No discussion' or 'Stop discussing'.

Another function which you must fulfil is ensuring that the members are fully aware of the subject they are brainstorming and a clarification of this subject. Different words can mean different things to a number of people, particularly if they are not clearly expressed. The brainstorming group is called together with an express purpose to generate ideas for the solution of 'X'. You must ensure that everybody knows exactly what is meant by 'X'. If not, the subject of the meeting must be clarified or re-clarified.

Your final function in the role of encourager is to take part in the meeting, showing that you are not restricted by barriers yourself, particularly that of perhaps making a fool of yourself.

Hiatus periods

During any brainstorming meeting, perhaps several times, silence falls because the members are unable to think of any more ideas. Usually by this stage the 'normal', logical suggestions have been made, but the members have not travelled too far along the path of creativity. You must not assume that this silence means that no more can be achieved. Instead, there are two actions you can take.

1 All the ideas will have been written on sheets of flipchart paper and fixed to the walls around the room. You can usefully read out all the ideas and, with the help of the recorder, total the number made to that stage. If, for example, 36 ideas have been offered, a simple encouragement to try for 40 can be made. This often results in 40 being exceeded in a flurry of ideas, so the numerical target can be repeated.
2 If it appears that creative ideas are slow in emerging, you might offer one or two rather wild ideas yourself
   (i) to show that you are willing to come out with this type of idea
   (ii) to encourage others to do the same.

The recorder

Someone to write down the ideas is needed, preferably a person who is not part of the group membership, otherwise one member's views might be lost in the difficult task of recording. It is advisable that the recorder is able to write both speedily and clearly. The contributions are written on sheets of flipchart paper as they are shouted out by the members. During this activity the recorder must ensure the following points:

• The contributions must be written down exactly as stated by the member.
• Every contribution, however silly it might appear, is recorded.
• Even though the recorder might not understand a contribution, the member should not be asked what he or she means.

The recorder will assist the chairperson at the periods of silence described above, and in fact may read the list at the chairperson's request, or may total for the chairperson the number of ideas recorded.

The form of a brainstorming meeting

A useful form of structure for a brainstorming meeting is now shown.

1 *State or restate the objective of the meeting* This statement will include the problem to be brainstormed, either as presented or as revised following discussion. It may be necessary to remind the members of the purpose of the brainstorming, that is to generate as many ideas as possible to help towards solving the problem.

2 *Describe the meeting structure* In most cases this will be a simple statement of the control rules during the brainstorming—no comments on or discussion of the ideas or suggestions proposed.

3 *Use a creativity encourager* Even if the members have previously taken part in brainstorming, every break between practice might enable some of the barriers to re-emerge. So it is useful to have at least one creative activity before the brainstorming proper commences.

4 *Restate the problem and start the brainstorming* Invite the members to throw in ideas for the recorder to write down on the paper available. The completed sheets should be fixed round the walls of the meeting room for all to see. Stated ideas can trigger other ideas, or half-thought-out ones can be developed. This process becomes much easier if the previous contributions are easily visible.

5 *Regenerate creativity* As suggested earlier, silences will fall at times during a session and may require your intervention. Experience suggests that the more creative ideas start flowing after the first main silence following the statement of the obvious ideas. The more the members are forced to produce ideas the more different the ideas that are likely to emerge, and these in turn can be developed into usable ones.

6 *Summarize* Although the completed sheets themselves are a summary, it is always useful for you to read aloud the final list. Even at this stage further ideas might emerge and it may be that one of these is the best one of the session. Thank the members for their participation and explain what is going to happen to the results of their brainstorming.

The organization of brainstorming meetings

Brainstorming needs little in the way of administration and requirements can be summarized as:

1 *Agenda* This is one of the occasions when not only is an agenda not issued beforehand, but even the subject to be discussed is not stated beforehand. Otherwise there is the danger that barriers might be constructed before the meeting. Foreknowledge of the subject will give members time to think about the suggestions that they would want to be accepted and this could blind them to other possibilities.

2 *Location* It is even more essential than in the case of the ordinary meeting that the brainstorming meeting should be held in isolation with no opportunity for any interruptions. Interruptions cause breaks in the thought processes and allow members to discuss ideas among themselves (rejecting some before they are even expressed). Isolation should present no problems as most brainstorming meetings are relatively short in duration.

3 *Timing* The length of time allocated to a brainstorm meeting will obviously depend on the subject, its complexity or its openness to the process. In general, most meetings of this nature last for 20 to 30 minutes and it will be often a useful strategy for you to impose a limit of this nature—the brain works faster under pressure! However, if at the end of the allotted time the ideas are still pouring out, the time can be extended without harm.

4 *Membership* Six to eight members is a useful size for a brainstorming meeting, although it can be held with fewer or more. If there are too few, there will be insufficient people to generate many ideas and the fewer the ideas, the less chance there will be that one idea will trigger at least one more. More than eight members might restrict the contribution potential of each member, particularly the quieter ones.

Much will depend on the culture and the size of the organization from which the members come, but in general the membership should be at peer level. With more senior members present, barriers may be constructed to avoid looking a fool, or one or more members may vie for the senior manager's praise by over-contributing. More junior members included in a membership of their bosses may feel inhibited or may over-contribute in the same way.

5 *Materials* All the materials necessary for the meeting must be on hand before the start of the meeting—paper, markers, drawing pins or adhesive material. Interruptions to replace, for example, a dried up marker pen can have the same bad consequences as any other interruption.

Decision making following brainstorming

As stated earlier, the purpose of brainstorming is to generate ideas, not to make decisions. Combining the decision-making process with that of problem solution seeking can have unfortunate results. However, a brainstorming meeting which has produced a vast number of ideas will have been wasted time if nothing is done with the ideas, and future meetings will cease to be effective.

The decision process

Once the ideas have been produced by the brainstorm meeting group, these ideas are then passed to the decision maker. This might be the same group that brainstormed the ideas; a completely different group; or one person who has the authority to make the decision. Whichever approach is used, the method will be similar in all cases.

1 Select from the list all the ideas that are obviously and immediately practicable.
2 Select the ideas which, although not immediately practicable, with some variation will become so.
3 Reject all the ideas which are so silly or so impractical that they would not be workable or desirable. Extreme care must be taken with these to ensure that the reasons for rejection are absolute and not flavoured by the decision maker's prejudices or narrowness of vision.
4 Select the ones which have been used previously and have been terminated. Consider whether circumstances have changed sufficiently to return them to the potential stage.
5 This will often leave a number of ideas which do not fall into the categories described above. These must be examined carefully and objectively for practicability.
6 The final list will contain
   (i) items which can be implemented
   (ii) items which require further investigation or development.
7 From the lists produced in (6), a decision is made on the idea/solution which is the most appropriate one in the circumstances, taking into account cost, resources, complexity, timing and all the other factors related to decision making and implementing.

Chapter 12

Large and formal meetings

Large meetings

Most of the meetings and techniques for handling them discussed so far have considered the meeting as being of a relatively small size—some eight to ten members or so as a maximum. This, of course, as far as you are concerned is the number for which to aim for maximum effectiveness and control as discussed so far.

However, there may be occasions when the membership numbers are beyond your control and a meeting with a large membership results. The large meeting has few differences in terms of preparation from the smaller meeting, except perhaps that you will need to take notice of rather different, possibly more exacting, environmental factors of seating, ventilation, etc. In a meeting with more than 12 or so members seating can become a difficulty and the various methods will have to be considered for appropriateness. Often the least acceptable arrangement of the theatre style has to be accepted.

The main problem can be that of control when there are a number of members exhibiting dysfunctional behaviours, usually the interrupters and those attempting to score points against other members in the room. The handling of these is the same as in the smaller meeting, although it becomes more difficult. In the classical large meeting, the House of Commons, the chairperson must take a stronger approach than would be usual in the smaller meeting and use more autocratic methods to suppress unwanted behaviour. This may not be politically acceptable in your meetings.

You will have less opportunity to become aware of the quiet members and opters-out. This is unfortunate, but is a fact of life in meetings of this nature—the more articulate, louder-voiced generally are able to make their points at the expense of others, unless you have an exceptionally good sense of awareness and can identify others who want to speak.

Interaction in meetings of this size becomes very difficult and they usually have to be conducted in a very formal and impersonal way if you are to maintain sufficient control. However, if interaction is necessary the buzz group approach can be utilized—I have used this effectively with an audience of 200 at a presentation and with large meetings smaller than this.

The meeting secretary

An invaluable approach to easing your burden in situations such as this is to provide support in the form of a meeting secretary. It is accepted that this will introduce yet another person to the meeting membership and involves you in yet more control and administration. However, in the types of cases cited above, these disadvantages are outweighed by the many advantages.

The secretary can take over from you the routine environmental tasks described earlier—arranging a meeting place, sending out invitations, arranging refreshments, etc. and be your additional 'right hand'. But an effective secretary can be utilized much more than in these routine ways and can make your control of the meeting so much easier—keeping notes of the proceedings, being aware of events you do not see, and so on. In short, an effective secretary can leave you free to concentrate on the principal duty of your role which is management of the progress of the meeting and the effective utilization of the members.

Few chairpersons, particularly when they are in charge of a meeting of more than eight or so members, can combine to the full necessary extent the roles of controlling the discussion and action on the task of the meeting, and controlling the behaviour of the members. Attempting this and at the same time trying to keep coherent notes of the meeting in order to summarize and produce action notes or minutes, produces an almost impossible task.

The role of the meeting secretary

The role of the meeting secretary can be summarized as follows:

1 *Pre-meeting* Support can be given to you in the early stages of arranging a meeting by a discussion of the potential agenda and the time needed to fulfil the agenda requirements. This is a particularly important support by the secretary if you are new to the role or the particular meeting.

The secretary can take over from you all or most of the administrative tasks relating to the meeting arrangement—sending out documents, chasing overdue reports, ensuring that subject speakers will be available, arranging the meeting room and all matters relating to it, arranging refreshments and other during-meeting requirements.

2 *During the meeting* The secretary's work can commence immediately before the meeting actually starts by helping you in the reception of the members, ensuring that all members have all the necessary papers, etc., and determining any special requirements.

The secretary's principal role during the meeting, however, will be keeping notes of the discussion, proposals, agreements, decisions in order to construct minutes or action notes. The secretary is usually the expert on the meeting procedures and regulations, if any, and is in a position to advise you if any points of order or difficulty arise.

Because the secretary will be constantly looking at the members to note who is speaking or proposing, etc., this will afford an excellent opportunity to be aware of members who are trying, but failing, to attract your eye, or perhaps who are showing other non-verbal signals. These behaviours can be quietly drawn to your attention.

Although the conventional role of the secretary is to maintain a low profile and usually speak only when invited to do so, or when a point of procedure arises, a more active role is possible. In certain circumstances it is necessary for a secretary's report to be given at the meeting—perhaps detailing actions since the previous meeting, statistics relevant to the organization, and so on. This can be done with the opportunity for the members to ask and the secretary to answer questions about the report.

Other more active participation can involve the reading of the minutes of the previous meeting (if this is part of the procedure) and also confirming apologies for absence.

A more involved role can occasionally be played when the secretary, because the contribution of a member may not have been clear or may have been incomplete, contributes to the meeting by posing a clarity probing question at the speaker. This will be especially relevant if the chairperson has failed to take up this important point, or the secretary can see looks of puzzlement on the faces of the members. The secretary, although interrupting the flow of the meeting, can be reasonably certain that if the speaker's contribution is not understood by the secretary, there is every likelihood that other members will be in the same position. So interruption is in this case helping the meeting process along.

But the principal part of the role remains the notetaking activity for eventual minute or action note production.

One final activity for which the secretary can be responsible and so support you, is to receive any incoming messages for members during the meeting and make the decision whether they are sufficiently urgent or important to be passed to the member during the meeting.

3 *After the meeting* The task of the secretary continues once the meeting has concluded. The principal task is obviously to convert the notes made during the meeting into the clear, coherent, concise notes or minutes required by the administration. These notes may produce a first draft for you to complete; a fair copy for you to amend in minor ways; or a discussion with you so that you can produce the notes/minutes. The secretary will then be responsible for circulating the notes either for the information of the members or for their confirmation or comments.

Because the secretary is in fairly constant contact with the members, one responsibility is often that of following up the proposed actions with the relevant members to ensure implementation, or at least producing a progress report for you.

Outside the actual meeting, the secretary is often responsible for controlling the filing of minutes/notes, reports and papers, making them available for reference by you or members on request. The post is the focal point for enquiries about the meeting system, and also for the submission of papers, etc.

The secretary can obviously be a powerful role in relation to the meeting and its system, much more powerful than the post appears to suggest. You can be guarded from undue interference and many minor items can be put into the responsibility area of the secretary rather than needing to be performed by you.

The structure of the large, formal meeting

Most of the rules, conventions and procedures described for the smaller meeting are applicable in the case of the larger, more formal type of meeting. Perhaps there is a greater degree of formality in the latter case with contributions being directed at or through the chair, rather than a more direct member-to-member interaction. There are usually more specific rules and procedures which have to be followed—these are necessary to avoid confusion during the meeting.

These strictures will obviously inhibit the meeting to some extent, reducing the freer flow of the smaller, more informal meeting, but considerable progress can still be made.

Decisions are usually produced as the result of a vote rather than by consensus agreement, and the vote majority may not necessarily reflect the value of the proposal, rather the p(P)olitical strength of the group supporting the proposal.

Depending on the organization and the requirements it places on meetings within it, the rules and regulations can be complex and widespread.

Order of business
There will usually be a specified order of business which has to be followed, requiring such items as apologies; minutes of the previous meeting (even if they have been circulated); discussion of matters arising from the minutes; correspondence; official reports, and so on to follow in sequence.

The quorum
In many formal meeting systems, either as an organizational or legal or quasi-legal requirement, a quorum is essential to allow the meeting to progress officially. This quorum is a number of members or percentage number of members required to be present before the meeting can be declared official. This might be 15 members from a total membership of 25, or it may be 51 per cent presence. If the quorum is not met, the meeting is basically invalid, although it can proceed on the basis that any 'decisions' will need to be ratified by a full meeting.

Proposals
Whereas in the more informal meeting a proposal by a member can be made unannounced during the meeting, in the formal meeting the proposal, or more usually a 'motion' has to be presented prior to the meeting in a written form. Whereas a proposal in an informal meeting usually arises as a result of discussion, the formal meeting takes completely the reverse approach. No discussion is allowed until the

motion has been proposed and seconded. The proposer is allowed to describe the motion, propose the motion, have it seconded, and then the members can discuss.

Changes to motions can be made only as 'amendments', which like the original motion need to be proposed and seconded before discussion, and there are often strict rules about who can speak and when in support of or against an amendment.

If an amendment is tabled, it must be cleared before any further action can be taken on the original motion. If the motion changes words or sentences in the original motion, and it is accepted by vote, the original motion is amended and this amended version becomes the motion before the meeting—the substantive motion.

During the discussion (or debate) of the motion, there are are frequently rules of debate imposed. During the debate, or indeed at any time during meetings of this nature, you as the chairperson have almost absolute control. Unless you are ignoring or negating the established rules and procedures, the chair has absolute control and requires total acceptance of this right.

This is particularly so in the structure of the debate. The intention should always be to follow as fair a pattern of discussion as possible, and to this end you have the right to determine this pattern. Members who express an interest in speaking will be called upon to state their views, and the fairest pattern is usually to have alternative speakers from the 'for' and 'against' lobbies.

This introduces the problem for chairperson and members of identifying the members who wish to contribute, their priorities and, from the members' point of view, being recognized as wishing to speak.

You will usually have a good knowledge of the power and responsibility level among the members and this knowledge can be utilized in determining the initial speakers when they signal they wish to speak. Otherwise, the principle must be that if the subject has been opened for debate, any member who wishes to speak should be allowed to do so.

Catching the chairperson's eye
Members of large meetings often have a problem of being recognized by the chair as wanting to speak. Sometimes the problem might be related to the seating of a member—the would-be contributor may be masked by a well-built member between you and him or her. But on many other

occasions the fault lies in the simple inability of the contributor to make effective signals and so 'catch the chairperson's eye', an important feature of this type of meeting.

The most obvious and widely used method is when one speaker finishes speaking, a member might speak out by saying 'Chair' or 'Mr/Madam Chairman' or some other acceptable formula, and so attract the attention of the chairperson. Unfortunately several members may do this at the same time and one will be recognized by the chair. Depending on the way in which a particular chairperson might be influenced, often the loudest or most impactive voice wins the right to speak. Very quiet, or quietly spoken members often suffer because of this. They consequently have to ensure by other means that they are recognized.

A useful approach which uses the power of non-verbal communication is for the member to make a hand movement to attract your attention, in addition to calling out. This, of course, is not infallible, because again other members may be doing the same thing! Other non-verbal signals include leaning forward so that they are clearly visible from the chair and also looking directly at you with what is often described as a 'meaningful look'.

A cluster of non-verbal signals is often a good approach taken:

- Leaning forward and rising slightly from your chair.
- Lifting one hand slightly and almost pointing.
- Opening the mouth slightly by starting to speak, but not actually speaking.
- Lifting the eyebrows slightly (although with many people this is automatic if the other actions are taken).
- Looking directly at the chairperson as these actions are taken.

Part of your control role will be to look out for such signals and take account of them in your control of the debate.

Some people recognize that they do not have the type of presence which will ensure that they are seen by the chairperson. With this recognition, but with the need to express their views, if there is a secretary it is a useful move for them to become known to that person and to explain the problems encountered. The secretary can become an ally when they wish to speak, by advising you of their request.

As chairperson, knowing that a number of disparate members will wish to speak on certain subjects, it can be valuable to work out or agree a strategy for the discussion pattern. This will help to avoid domination by the 'powerful' or vocal members. Many committees have standing rules which describe the desirable approach, but if this is not the case, if you are a new chairperson of an existing meeting group, or a new meeting group, this can be the subject of discussion at an early meeting.

Points of procedure

People who are not accustomed to the processes of the formal meeting are often annoyed by what can be a frequent interruption on a 'point of order'. A member, during the debate, may, on this occasion without invitation, interrupt the speaker or chairperson by making the statement 'A point of order'. This interruption takes priority over the debate of the topic and must be dealt with before the debate can continue—if indeed this is possible. Many points of order raise the question whether the subject is for debate or debate by that meeting.

The point of order interruption is made when it appears that the rules and procedures are being ignored or mistreated. Used correctly this action can be helpful to you and the meeting and can assist you to direct the debate along acceptable lines.

But there is no doubt that the technique is misused as a tactic to delay a debate, to stop debate on a sensitive subject, to delay the meeting to gain time, and so on. The users of this tactic rely on the overriding power of the point of order and it is very difficult for the chairperson to avoid the interruptions. The points of order in cases of this nature are often incorrect: if you recognize this tactic, a definitive statement can be made about sanctions against the use of the procedure incorrectly.

Many other points of procedure exist and if you are to become a chairperson of a group which holds meetings in this style you must learn the formulae—the traditional statements or proposals which can be used. It is necessary to know what happens when they are used, and how to use them effectively and intelligently.

Voting

One other major difference between the smaller, informal and the larger, more formal meeting is that in the latter decisions are usually ratified by a vote.

A number of methods of voting can be used, but the most common one is a show of hands on the basis of one person, one vote. You will at the end of the debate on a motion call for a vote by show of hands by asking for an indication of those 'For the motion' and 'Against the motion'. The hands are counted and the majority carries the decision, either for or against the motion. Commonly there are also a number of members who vote neither way and will be recorded as abstainers if that is the particular rule of the meeting. Otherwise they will be ignored and it will be left to anyone who is interested to calculate the number of abstentions from the votes cast and the number at the meeting.

A variation of the 'one person, one vote' approach can be a 'card' or block voting system. In this case, one person represents an organization which has a particular voting value. The value of that block is taken into account in the vote counting—there may be only 20 members present at the meeting, but if each has a card representation, the actual voting may result in 1000 'for' (10 members with cards of value 100 each) and 500 'against' (10 members with cards of value 50 each). This approach is more common in political or trade union meetings where membership is more representational of groups rather than individual memberships.

The open vote in which all can see who is voting for, against or abstaining is the most common method, but on occasions and for particular subjects determined by the rules, a secret vote can be taken. As the name implies, in this case members record their votes in secret, usually by entering their decision on pieces of paper which are counted to identify the voting result. This is the method used, of course, in Britain's biggest meeting—the election poll. In many organizations this method of voting is usually applied when action has to be taken at a personal level—the appointment of a chairperson, the action against an individual member, and so on.

The advance of electronics has invaded the world of meetings. Instead of signifying your vote by a show of hands or an entry on a piece of paper, the vote is recorded by pressing a button on a small keyboard held by each member. The result is an electronically counted vote which might be displayed in detail with members' names, or may simply show an anonymous voting decision.

Whichever method of voting is used, there is always the possibility that the 'fors' and 'againsts' turn out to be equal in number. There are several ways of dealing with this, but particularly at the first of a series of new meetings, a decision must be made about the method of resolution. Sometimes it is agreed that when the vote is taken, you, the chairperson, will have no vote, but in the case of a 'hung' vote, you will have a vote which is effectively a casting vote. Or you may have a vote, but in the case of a balanced result have a second, casting vote. Considerable confusion can result if the specific method is not clarified for all.

So there can be a number of significant differences between the approaches and techniques used in formal and informal meetings, although the basic approaches of people control are very similar. The large formal meeting is becoming less the norm in favour of more democratic meetings, but there are still many meetings which, by law or internal rules, must follow the formal practice. There are a number of definitive publications on the practice of formal meetings and committees which can be referred to if necessary. One or two examples of these publications are included in the recommended reading list at the end of the book.

Law and meetings

The subject of the law relating to meetings is too extensive and complex to be covered in a book of this nature. However, many meetings are covered by some aspect or other of law and the chairperson and secretary in particular should be aware of these applications. Not every application can be recalled by a chairperson/secretary who is not a lawyer, but the principal ones and the need to refer in other cases should be known.

Meetings may be covered by common law, criminal law, statutes, local by-laws and regulations based on Acts. In addition, of course, there are the rules imposed by the organization in which the meeting is held. These are often not legal requirements directly, but can have an indirect link with a legal position to uphold them. An example of this is the Companies Acts which include direction on the holding of meetings. These regulations usually apply mainly to meetings of shareholders (initial statutory and subsequent annual and extraordinary general meetings) and some aspects of board meetings.

The most common legal proceedings resulting from meetings are concerned with the behaviour of members during the meeting. In such cases both criminal and civil law might be relevant. It is only in Parliament and the courts that the laws of libel and slander are covered by privilege. In meetings, slander, which is generally spoken, can generate legal proceedings and you must be alert to conflicts arising which might degenerate to the exchange of slanderous statements. In meeting cases there will normally be no lack of witnesses to the offence!

Chairpersons, secretaries and members of the majority of meetings which are small and informal need not worry too much about legal aspects, except perhaps the slander aspects cited above. But officers of formal or official committees or meetings must know which legal covers exist and how they might affect the meeting practice.

PART TWO

Chapter 13

Being a member

Behaviour of members

Unless the members themselves take an active part, no meeting can succeed. After all, the purpose of calling a meeting is to give the members the opportunity to participate and work together towards the aims of the meeting.

But the members must behave in an effective manner to attain these aims. Earlier we considered the findings of Rackham and Morgan (1977) in the behaviour of chairmen and members in effective meetings. Table 13.1 repeats the analysis figures produced from these studies.

Table 13.1 Behaviour profiles of meetings

Category	Behaviour by chairmen (%)	Behaviour by others (%)
Content proposals	1.8	11.1
Procedural proposals	9.6	2.4
Building	3.2	2.0
Supporting	5.8	15.5
Disagreeing	2.0	8.4
Defending/attacking	0.1	1.1
Testing understanding	15.2	3.1
Summarizing	11.5	0.7
Seeking information	28.1	16.3
Giving information	21.7	39.4

Source: Rackham and Morgan (1977).

The analysis in Table 13.1 shows the effective behaviour profiles of meetings for both chairpersons and members. As far as the members are concerned, the high percentage, 39.4 per cent, of giving information reflected this purpose of holding a meeting and using the membership actively. Between one-third and one-half of all the member contributions were concerned with their providing information, views, opinions and feelings; 11.1 per cent, the fourth highest category, was concerned with the members offering proposals for the content of the meeting which, with 2 per cent building, represents a substantial amount of the total contributions.

Supporting behaviour between members is high, 15.5 per cent in effective meetings, with a correspondingly lower percentage of disagreeing, 8.4 per cent. This latter behaviour is natural, since many decisions which would not have otherwise been made, stem from disagreement. The Rackham figures do not show whether the reasons for disagreement were stated; my own analyses of effective meetings show the largest part of these disagreements do have the reasons stated: less effective meetings have a higher proportion of bald, unreasoned disagreement. A high percentage, 16.3 per cent, of questions was asked, naturally where members care what the others think and feel.

Consequently, the profile of an effective meeting member is one with high percentages of contribution in

- giving information, opinions, views and feelings
- content proposals
- supportive behaviour
- seeking the views of others.

The profile is low on

- disagreements, although they do exist,
- the negative behaviours of defending/attacking.

A broader analysis would also have shown a low occurrence of

- blocking behaviour
- interrupting
- disagreeing without giving reasons.

And a high occurrence of

- bringing-in.

Meetings which fit this profile to a reasonable extent have a very good likelihood of being successful and effective.

The proposer
One of the most effective behaviours of a member is proposing.
Obviously not every member can or wants to put forward proposals and too many proposals can cause problems. But if the members are willing to make proposals this shows that they are prepared to share their views in public and make positive statements for action. This is the type of behaviour which a meeting needs. Care must be taken by the chairperson not to lean too heavily on the member who appears to be the most prolific proposer as the danger can be that the rest of the group will opt out.

The builder
Although even in effective meetings building behaviour occurs at a low level only, it can be considered as possibly the most important behaviour. Building on the suggestions or proposals made by others requires that:

- People listen to the proposals made.
- Consideration of their value is given.
- They can and should be supported.
- They might be improved.

Almost any proposal considered in-depth can be improved and consequently building can take place. The behaviour is obviously relatively rare because most people have a high degree of self-centring and are interested only in pushing their own ideas.

The supporter
The Rackham figures show a substantial degree of supporting in an effective meeting. Too often when a member complains that there was no support the other members reject this claim saying that they said nothing because they did not disagree. Support is rarely recognized as support unless it is expressed verbally and the person supported is aware of it. Even non-verbal support—smiling, nodding—should be accompanied by verbal support because the person supported may not be looking that way to see the non-verbal signal. Silence does not mean agreement or assent: all it means is that the people concerned are not taking active steps to say what they feel.

The compromiser

The effective meeting member must be prepared to show a high degree of compromise. Most proposals can be improved in some way, often by quite drastic surgery. The initiator must be prepared to give way on certain aspects if he or she is convinced that in so doing the initial proposal will be strengthened. This requires compromise.

On occasions, members need to compromise their views and show that they are willing to yield for the sake of progress. This does not mean that they must betray their firm views or their conviction that what they are proposing is in the best interests: all members must be in a role of potential compromiser. So there will obviously be times to yield and times to stand fast—a stubborn approach can have disastrous effects. But there must not be constant yielding because this can be indicative of non-assertiveness on the part of the yielders and aggressiveness on the part of the member(s) to whom yielded.

Membership effectiveness

There are a number of ways in which you can become more effective as a meeting member. Some of the important aspects are:

- Attendance requirements
- Self-preparation
- Personal objectives
- Agenda items
- Proposals

Attendance

The first question to ask when you receive an invitation to attend a meeting is 'Should I go?' To determine the answer you should then ask:

- What is the agenda for the meeting and what are the objectives?
- Are these objectives in line with my interests and responsibilities?
- Will my interests, those of my department or organization be furthered by my attendance?
- Will the achievements be worth the expenditure of my time?
- Can all the same results be achieved in any other way?
- Will I be able to contribute anything of value to the meeting?
- Would the meeting be any less effective without my contributions (no false modesty!)?

The next question should then be 'Should I go?' Have you a deputy or other member of your staff who can represent you effectively? Perhaps it is even more relevant for a deputy to attend rather than you. Is there someone else who is not your second in command, but whom you are trying to develop through a coaching plan which includes attending some of your meetings?

Your representative must be fully briefed and aware of the parameters of his or her authority and responsibility. On too many occasions representation is preceded by the boss throwing the agenda to the person concerned with the requirement to 'go to this meeting for me'. This can also result in disagreements after the meeting because the representative did not say certain things or take certain actions—unfortunately he or she was insufficiently briefed prior to the meeting regarding action to be taken.

You should give a thorough briefing so that your representative has a clear idea of

- why he or she is going
- what is expected of him or her
- what action will be required on his or her return from the meeting.

The agenda should be considered in detail with the representative:

- What do the agenda items mean?
- Which ones are of particular significance to you?
- What action is he or she expected to take in relation to each item?
  - Keep quiet?
  - Join the free discussion?
  - Make a proposal? What is the proposal and what is the consideration behind it? How strongly should it be made?
  - Should the proposer back down for any particular counter-proposal? Who is likely to be the strongest competitor? To what extent should building take place?
  - Support certain proposals? What proposals does the boss know will be made? What reaction should the representative have to these proposals? How strong should these reactions be?
- How far does the representative's authority stretch to make decisions at the meeting or to vary the points discussed above?
- What authority can he or she quote for decisions made?

- How detailed a report-back do you want? Orally or in writing? When do you want it?

In this way the representative will attend the meeting with much more confidence than simply being sent 'as the representative', and will be able to make a much more effective contribution to the process of the meeting.

Self-preparation

If you are to attend the meeting yourself, your preparation for it should be almost as extensive as that described for the chairperson, because the action of you and the other members will determine to a large extent the effectiveness of the meeting. This preparation will also determine how effective you will be in achieving your personal objectives for attending the meeting.

Personal objectives

These might simply be described as the items on the agenda, but few members attend a meeting with only these as their objectives. Within each objective or agenda item, what do you want to achieve? It may be that you might have a passing interest only in some of the items, or they are not sufficiently important to you other than to take part in any discussion on them and share your knowledge and experience, or help to find solutions. In this latter case, it will certainly be useful to think about the item and consider what you know and how this might be related to the item. But there will be certain items in which you will have a strong interest and will be attending the meeting with every intention of ensuring that your proposals for action in these areas are accepted.

Agenda items

Read the agenda thoroughly and also read what may be behind the agenda items! Ensure that you understand what each item is intended to cover: if it is not clear, find out before the meeting what it is. You might find that if you left this until the meeting itself, a surprise twist might be forced on you, one for which you are not prepared and consequently with which you may not be able to cope as you would have wished. Identify which items have importance for you as suggested above. If you have an additional item for the agenda, one which is sufficiently urgent and important to be included in this meeting, ensure that the chairperson is aware of the item well before the meeting so that there is every opportunity for it to be added to the agenda.

Read carefully any papers which accompany the agenda to ensure that you understand them, and you are aware of any relevance or interest to you. Be particularly careful over long papers, especially if the writer normally produces short, impactive reports: often this length suggests either the writer is not committed to the content, or within it there is hidden a sting for which you should be prepared.

Proposals

The most care and attention in preparation that you should take will obviously be concerned with any proposals you intend to make.

- Be absolutely certain about the reasons for, background to and details of the proposal you intend to put forward.
- Research and have available any data necessary to support your proposal.
- Decide whether you should inform the meeting members beforehand about the proposal. If you do, will this give them time to think up arguments against the proposal? If you do not, this will allow you to spring a surprise on them, but it will not have given them time to consider the proposal realistically and perhaps even support it!
- Write down the proposal and adjust the words until it is as short, clear and impactive as possible and couched in oral, rather than written language. Memorize the proposal wording so that when the time comes to offer it, it will come out naturally and as you meant it to do. The kinds of proposal which are usually badly received are the ones which are presented in a hesitant, woolly and unclear manner. Give your proposal the best presentational chance it can have. have.
- Consider the possible arguments which might be made against it and rehearse the responses to these. It is much more effective to prepare for too many arguments than too few and be caught unawares.

At the meeting

Attending

Ensure that you are at the meeting about five minutes or so before it is due to start. It is only polite not to be late for the start of a meeting, and after all, if you are late and the meeting has started, you may have missed something of importance to you.

Your role

It may be that in your preparation for the meeting you decided that to ensure that you achieve certain objectives, you will have to take on a particular role. The roles that members take have been discussed earlier, particularly in the way that chairpersons might deal with them.

- Are you going to take a supportive role in certain instances, perhaps so that you will be supported in turn?
- Are there items with which you will disagree? If so, how are you going to disagree, remembering that behaviour breeds behaviour and the way in which you treat other people will probably affect the way they treat you.

Considering in advance how you are going to act may seem a cold-blooded and unrealistic way of behaving. But it is usually better to be prepared for actions and reactions, rather than to try to react when they happen. If you had not previously considered it, you might be taken completely unawares and thrown off your tracks by a surprise disagreement or objection. Of course, there will be times when you will have to react to an unexpected event, but even in cases such as this the rule must be not to react without thinking—even a moment's thought may produce the effective reaction rather than blundering into a conflict situation.

Presenting a proposal

If you have a proposal to present, you will have decided beforehand what you are going to say and how you are going to present it.

- Do not be hesitant in your presentation.
- Do not present in an over-dominant or patronizing manner.
- Speak clearly and carefully so that your proposal is heard and understood.
- 'Sell' rather than 'tell'.
- In most cases it will be better to sell the benefits of your proposal rather than its features—'What's in it for people?'
- Support your proposal with its major arguments, retaining lesser arguments as support for the proposal if there is disagreement.
- Be prepared to discuss the advantages and benefits of your proposal if it is challenged, but do not argue. If it is possible, have papers or data sheets to support arguments and hand these out at the relevant

times—the other members will probably be impressed by your efficiency or will be taken unawares.

- If you need further support, bring in other members whom you have lobbied prior to the meeting and who have agreed to support you.
- Keep to the point in your discussion—you will not help your case by rambling or introducing red herrings.
- Respect the views of others and their rights to express these, even if they disagree with your own.
- Avoid sarcasm when responding and do not belittle the arguments of others—this will only serve to make them more antagonistic to your ideas.
- Be ready to recognize attitudes and feelings, particularly to realize when it is a waste of time pursuing a certain course. Accept the position if you have to without giving the appearance of sulking or being hurt (even though internally this is exactly how you feel).
- If you have nothing further to say, shut up. Little will be achieved by extending arguments and repeating them when it is obvious that they were heard and understood the first time round.

Although it may not help to have your views accepted, a minimum of personalization will reduce any antagonism towards them. Avoid giving too many 'I' examples, although some will ensure that the other members know that you are committed to your proposals or views. Certainly avoid the 'When we did this . . .' or 'When I was at . . .' approaches on too many occasions.

Listening
When you have nothing to say, keep quiet and listen to what others are saying. People have said to me that often they use these non-talking periods to rehearse in their mind what they are going to say—in important aspects, these thoughts should have occurred prior to the meeting in self-preparation time. If you are thinking deeply, you cannot be listening actively and may miss something of value. While others are speaking, their thoughts might trigger new/better ideas in your mind or perhaps ways in which you can build on their proposals to improve these. Listening may also enable you to identify problems which others have not seen because they were too immersed in their own ideas.

Many people find it difficult to listen to others for extended periods, particularly if the views being expressed are complex. Just sitting looking at the speaker is an excellent recipe for being seen with eyes glazing over.

Take notes in cases like this, even if they are not necessary. By having to concentrate on what to put down in your notes, you will concentrate more on what the speaker is saying. A useful method is to practise the patterned notetaking technique popularized by Tony Buzan (1974, 1988). This helps you to concentrate on the key points being made by the speaker without having to do too much writing for the notes.

Do not interrupt, even if there is something about which you are not clear. The speaker may clarify the point later on, but if not make a note of the question you wish to pose. A note of the point will help you to remember it, particularly if a little later another point of doubt arises. By the time the speaker has finished, you may not be able to remember without a written prompt all the points you wished to raise. How many times, after a situation has passed, have you thought to yourself 'I wanted to ask about . . . and now it's too late.'

Ask questions if you do not understand. This will give the speaker the opportunity to clarify points which perhaps others too have not understood, and it certainly lets the speaker know you have been listening. Do not allow vague or unclear statements to pass without challenge—sometimes these are ploys used by proposers to insert important points which might otherwise create disagreement or argument. Ask probing questions so the proposer is aware that you want to know everything before you either support him or her or disagree.

Unless there are very good reasons for doing so—and these can be rare in a group where relationships are good—do not engage in 'game playing' as meetings are ideal places for this.

Game playing

The concept of playing behavioural or psychological 'games' originated in the model known as Transactional Analysis, a social model of behaviour introduced by Eric Berne (Berne, 1964). The model originated in psychotherapy but Berne extended its use into wider fields of more 'normal' behaviour. Transactional Analysis (TA) includes the identification of roles and behaviours, and explains such life incidents as procedures and rituals, life scripts, pastimes, and so on. It also introduces the concept of 'games people play'.

These games, usually played when the people concerned are in the 'Child' mode of behaviour, are many and varied and are usually destructive, however pleasant some of them may appear to be. Many of them can be seen to be played in meetings, usually to the detriment of the meeting.

A typical game is NIGYSOB which stands for 'Now I've Got You You Sonofabitch'! The incident starts at a meeting when, consciously or unconsciously, one member hurts another, perhaps by ridiculing a proposal or opinion. The result of this can be that the hurt member's motivation is now centred on retaliation. This may result in the situation when the next meeting is called that the hurt member goes to that meeting, not with any commitment to the meeting other than to 'get' the member who hurt him or her. All this member's energy in the meeting is directed towards this objective and results in a high feeling when it is achieved—NIGYSOB! But unfortunately, this is rarely the end of the matter. The other member now has become the victim and can determine to 'get' the persecutor. The process then becomes a 'game' which can have disastrous results for the two players, the onlookers and the meeting, until something happens to end the game.

Another group game which is used in meetings is 'Why Don't you—yes but'. One person will approach the meeting with a problem for which he or she cannot find a solution. With the intention of being helpful a member might suggest a 'Why don't you . . .' solution, to which the response is 'Yes, that sounds good, but . . .'. The first suggestion having been rejected, another member makes a suggestion which receives the same response. And so the game goes on until the members realize the problem-owner has no intention of accepting any suggestions and stop making them. Whereupon the problem-owner goes away, thinking or saying 'Well I didn't expect you to come up with anything useful. I suppose I'll just have to solve it myself as I always do.'

The basic result of these games is that at least one person is hurt—the victim—and another person develops a self-righteous feeling of either winning or being rejected. Neither result is healthy and if games of this nature, and the many others possible, are played at meetings, the meeting as a whole suffers.

The advice is simple—do not initiate games or if someone else tries to involve you, refuse to play. NIGYSOB only succeeds as a game if both parties decide to 'get' the other; 'Yes but' succeeds for the persecutor if the victims do not quickly realize what is happening and refuse to satisfy the persecutor's advances. And so with the other games. It takes more than one person to play a game, or to make it work for the persecutor or voluntary victim. If you start a game, be prepared for the worst consequences, because nobody wins. The simple advice is to avoid game playing.

The dirty tricks department

My objective in including this section is not to commend that you indulge in dirty tricks to satisfy your meeting objectives. But life is not all sweetness and light and others will be playing games and taking actions which are not straightforward. The effective member should be able to recognize what is happening and take the necessary action—as with game playing. However, I am not so naïve to suggest that even the most effective member will not indulge in a 'dirty trick' sometimes to achieve an objective, and there may even be occasions and situations when it is necessary to do so. This is not to condone the analogy of 'in a world of blind people, the one-eyed man is king', but in the words of a popular song of some years back 'sometimes you've got to fight to be a man!'

Planned aggression

The rejection or non-reaction to aggression and conflict has been discussed earlier and the recommendation that you use neither of these yourself. However, there may be occasions when this may be the appropriate strategy to achieve your objectives. It must be recognized, however, that this approach will be at the expense of other people who will almost certainly realize (too late to do anything at the time) what you have done, and will be suspicious of you at subsequent meetings. Or they may even decide to play the game of NIGYSOB.

Getting angry or escalating an event to conflict in a deliberate and controlled manner works best when this type of behaviour is not your normal behaviour. Adroitly used it can be very effective, but you must give no indication that it was simulated, nor later admit it was simulated, otherwise nobody will believe your anger again.

Even within your anger there are rules to follow. Although your anger is addressed at another, do not personalize your attack, keep it aligned on the 'thing'. Otherwise, the more likely reaction is for someone o defend himself or herself and react with even more aggression and conflict.

The aim must be surprise—surprise in the speed and level of your offensive. Your comments must be brief, authorative and impactive, delivered in a cool, almost unemotional voice. But to be really effective the attack must not be signalled in advance. When you have prepared yourself to move, do so with speed and without warning. Do not maintain your offensive too long—as soon as you see you have made your point or the others realize your commitment and start accepting, back away (not down) and be ready to compromise (but only within the limits you have previously decided on). At this stage, as in negotiating, it is a useful strategy to make false concessions, concessions which you would have made in any case if anybody had asked for them. This suggests you are no longer angry and are willing to compromise or withdraw your attack, now that it has succeeded.

Delaying tactics

At times it is in your interest as a member for a decision not to be made, or not to be made immediately and you therefore need to delay its progress. There are a number of approaches, several of which were described in Chapter 9, concerned with the chairperson's control of dysfunctional members. If you have a very astute and strong chairperson your delaying task is going to be so much more difficult; in other circumstances, the meeting does not stand a chance!

Disagreement will always extend a discussion without causing apparent problems as long as the disagreement is not violent. But the discussion to try to win over your disagreement, particularly if it was unexpected, will eat into the time available. Always be prepared to contain this delaying discussion within a reasonable period, but it can always be refreshed by your appearing to accept the arguments, then returning to the point a short while afterwards by saying 'I've been thinking about what you said about . . ., but another point has occurred to me' (this point can even be one which has already been covered).

Red herrings thrown in, particularly if you make them not too distant from the subject under discussion, can be time wasters. There is the time you take in introducing the red herring; the time taken by the chairperson perhaps in trying to get the discussion back on track; the time taken when you try to reintroduce the red herring—one attempt is rarely successful or worth while; any time taken by the meeting in discussing the diversion; and the further time taken by the chairperson in trying to regain control. Red herrings can be taken from a range of subjects, but they are much more likely to be taken up if they are (a) not too distant from the interrupted subject and (b) subjects which you know interest a number of members. The best long-term procrastinator is to have a subject referred for investigation by an expert or a sub-committee. The initial stages in this are to question (not state) whether the members of the meeting have all the expertise and knowledge to be able to pronounce on the subject. The raising of complex and complicated technical issues can often help here provided they can be made to appear very relevant. Once some doubt has been cast in the members' minds, suggest that it could be less risky to refer the subject to a sub-group or sub-committee or expert for a report-back to this group (who of course would be the final arbiters). Notice will be taken if you can quote an acknowledged expert as 'the sort of person we could ask for advice'. If you put yourself in the apparent position of certainly not knowing everything about the subject and needing the advice of others, other members are hardly likely to say they know everything (even if they do).

An extension of this ploy will be to ensure that you are elected to the sub-committee itself, so that you can influence the way it goes about its task. This is usually quite easy to achieve because, as you are prepared to attend yet another meeting (to achieve your aim), other members may not be as keen to do so.

Let's put it in writing

This is another ploy to take control of a situation and ensure that your objectives are achieved. During the discussions which take place in a meeting there may be one which is part of your personal agenda to achieve in a particular way. The agreement appears to be going in a way contrary to your preferred result. Before the agreement becomes too obvious, you can raise several difficulties and suggest strongly that this subject will require more discussion than the meeting obviously has time for (even if this is not the case, it is unlikely that you will be challenged). Immediately suggest that a paper be written giving the advantages and disadvantages for consideration by the next meeting. This suggestion should be immediately followed up with the comment that you would be prepared to produce such a paper.

The chairperson and other members may be on a spot. Even though they feel the subject may soon be tied up, they have had the suspicion raised that it may be more difficult than they were thinking. Your offer may place them in a quandary—if they said 'no' they might appear to be being churlish towards a member, one of whose objectives was helping the meeting. Once you have the authority to write the paper, the means is in your hands to produce something which if not completely forcing the decision to your side, strongly (but carefully) supports it to an extent that other approaches appear less effective. This is equivalent to the concept that 'the hand that writes the minutes, controls the meeting'.

There are many more strategies that members use in meetings to get their own way, but usually these involve cutting down other people in some way and I do not commend these at all. Hassling other members and the chairperson; casting indirect doubts on a member's knowledge or even veracity; making others uncomfortable in a variety of ways—these are all aggressive strategies which can work. However, because they hurt people, these people determine not to be hurt again, and either the meetings suffer or you find that the barriers against you are built too high for you to achieve anything ever again—even if now you are wanting to help the meeting. Interactive appropriateness is usually built on effective relationships and assertive–responsive behaviour, rather than aggression.

Meetings in other countries

More and more people, now that the international scene from the Americas, through Europe to the Far East is becoming more of an active market, are travelling from this country to attend meetings elsewhere, whether these are sales meetings with potential buyers, negotiations over contracts and agreements, or meetings with the continental parent company which has bought the company in another country. This, of course, is not a new phenomenon—business people have always travelled, albeit not so frequently nor so extensively. However, the atmosphere is changing and the former almost universal use of, for example, English is reducing. Some business people have been heard to say to their English counterparts 'If I come to sell to you, I will speak English; if you come to my country to sell to me, I shall expect you to speak my language.' Fortunately other countries are still quite condescending to the British and Americans and will speak English if there is no alternative. But this situation will not continue at this level permanently and business people who intend to take full advantage of the world market must attempt to learn other languages. If a language or languages can be learned to a level sufficient to carry out a business meeting, this is the ideal aim. But below this level, just as we appreciate other nationals making an effort to learn a little of our language, so other nationalities are delighted (albeit sometimes amused) when foreigners attempt their language.

To see the situation of the use of other languages, we can refer to a number of language surveys of recent years. One, conducted in 1989 by *Eurobarometer* (a European Commission publication), showed that the people who had a working knowledge of other languages included the following:

Luxemburgers	10% with one other language	89% with two or more
Dutch	29% with one other language	44% with two or more
Belgians	22% with one other language	27% with two or more
Germans	33% with one other language	7% with two or more
French	26% with one other language	7% with two or more
Spanish	26% with one other language	6% with two or more
Portuguese	14% with one other language	10% with two or more
—	—	—
British	20% with one other language	6% with two or more
Irish (Eire)	17% with one other language	3% with two or more

Every race and culture has its own attitude to meeting procedures, methods and behaviour and we must be aware of these differences if we are to make our encounters effective. Not only are there differences between cultures, but the differences between one culture and another may not be the same as between that culture and another different one.

If you are to take part in a meeting, formal or informal, between two or more cultures it is obviously in your interest to learn about the meeting mores of the races with whom you are dealing. Errors and gaffes are acceptable at a first or unique meeting, but become less so over a series of them. No longer can the participant expect others to accept his or her native tongue all the time with no reciprocal attempts being made to move towards the other language. Even a little helps.

Chapter 14

Aids to contributions

Meetings are essentially about words. These words might be statements of information, view, opinion, feeling, support, disagreement, attacking, defending, interrupting, sarcasm, humour or any of the other verbal expectations used by people. More particularly at meetings they can be proposals made by a member who wants to ensure that

- the contribution is listened to
- the proposal is considered
- the proposal is accepted for implementation.

Earlier we considered how a member might make more positive and impactive contributions to the meeting. These approaches concentrated on the verbal approach, but the words can be successfully supplemented by effective pictures.

It is not the purpose of this book to give a full guide to presentational skills as there are many excellent, comprehensive works on the subject. When a meeting member starts to put forward a proposal, he or she becomes a presenter and should behave as an effective example of this using both words and pictures to make impact. Care must be taken not to overdo the use of aids and reliance must not be placed on them to replace the verbal proposal. If the proposal is supported by one overhead transparency slide after another in an unending stream, however well produced, the other members may either switch off or interrupt with an attacking behaviour. There is also the major problem if the proposer relies completely on OHP slides to project the message, rather than on the verbal presentation, and the electricity or the OHP fails!

Visual or aural aids are simply that, aids to support a verbal presentation.

Should presentational aids be used?

The implied importance of the use of aids cannot be accepted without question—several questions in fact!

- Will the use of visual aids enhance the presentation of the session?
- Will the use of visual aids assist the audience in understanding the presentation content?
- Have I the skills to make/obtain/use the visual aids deemed necessary?
- Which types of visual aids will be the most relevant?
- How many will I need?
- When would I use them?

Presentations of proposals have fallen on a number of occasions because of the inappropriate or ineffective use of aids.

Presentational aids available

The most important aids available for use in presentations include the following:

- The object itself (machine, set of procedures, etc.)
- The flipchart
- The whiteboard
- The chalkboard
- The overhead projector
- The transparency projector
- The audio-visual unit
- The audio cassette player
- The video player and the film projector

In meeting presentations all these aids can be used at one time or another, in different circumstances, but the ones which are more commonly used on these occasions are as follows:

- The object
- The flipchart or whiteboard
- The overhead projector (OHP)
- The video player

Many people tend to consider a presentation without aids as one which will not succeed—this is quite untrue. At the other extreme some presenters use almost every type of aid within the presentation. This usually results in them switching frantically between the OHP, the audio player, the flipchart, the video player, and so on—an orchestration of aids. Beware. There is a law which states that if anything can go wrong, there is every likelihood that it will; and a multi-aid, all singing–all dancing presentation is inviting the law to be imposed! One aid used effectively can have more impact than a plethora of aids with little impact.

Visual aid common features

There are a number of common features of use with a range of visual aids, including posters (flipcharts), chalkboards, whiteboards, overhead projector transparencies and to some extent 35 mm slides. The common factors among all these media are that they all have to be prepared, either manually or by means of a computer, for presentation use and can be used in a variety of ways.

The preparation factors include the lettering for text, the graphics for image presentation, colouring of both text and graphics, and the amount of material to include on one aid.

Depending on the medium used, the variety of ways in which these aids can be used includes the simple progressive entries on the aid, pre-prepared additive entries, subtractive methods and moving presentation. The pre-prepared aid is more common in presentations and consideration will be concentrated on this, but if you are an experienced and skilled visual aid user, considerable impact can be achieved by on-the-spot production.

Lettering

Flipcharts or transparencies of various kinds should present, in a size which can be seen by the meeting members, material which supports the words used by the presenter. The first hurdles to be overcome by the inexperienced presenter producing visual aids are how much to include and how to present the decided material.

The simple answer to 'How much?' is 'As little as possible'. If the aid is overloaded with words, there will probably be too much for the viewer to accept. If the aid contains very little, the question may be asked whether it was worth making the aid. On occasions, if an OHP transparency contains one word only, this starkness will make an impact on the audience. This may be true in some circumstances, but not necessarily in all. As suggested above, the reaction might in fact be negative in terms of 'Why show just that? He could have simply said that word! What a waste of a transparency!, etc.'

Compare the two transparencies demonstrated in Figures 14.1 and 14.2.

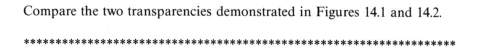

****

RECRUITMENT

****

Figure 14.1 Recruitment visual aid 1

****

RECRUITMENT

****

Figure 14.2   Recruitment visual aid 2

In Figure 14.2 a more effective use of the aid has been made with larger lettering, not only because it will be seen from a greater distance, but because a more effective use has been made of the 'white space'. If the larger word was to be printed on perhaps the diagonal instead of the horizontal, even larger lettering could have been used. If strong colouring had been included, the impact could have been even greater.

But the question must still be asked 'Is it necessary to have an aid of this nature at all?' There may be very good reasons for doing so, but on so many occasions the aid is produced without realistic consideration.

Size of lettering
Size is important and must relate directly to the size of the meeting group and the size of the meeting room. The lettering must be of a size so it can be read easily, even from the back of the room.

Distance from the aid
A distance of about 10 metres can be considered an absolute maximum and to ensure visibility over this range the lettering should be 5 cm tall, whether on a flipchart or projected image. But the size of the lettering is not the only criterion for visibility.

Number of words
As we discussed earlier, the number of words can make a considerable difference. I have found that the most effective posters have entries consisting of two or three words on each line with about six to eight lines in total. This amount is usually sufficient to act as reminders of or pointers to the more expanded verbal explanation of the presenter. But on many occasions this guidance has to be ignored and severe criticism is often academic because the psychology of an image has been determined in terms of so many words. You must decide, if the aid will contain much more than this, whether you should:

- Try to reduce the wording to shorthand
- Produce more than one aid to include the material
- Accept the numerous words and lines, but use other techniques to reduce the inappropriateness (e.g. the subtractive or additive techniques to be described later).

Colours
The use of colours in visual aids can be criticized in that: (a) the use of the colours becomes more important in the aid producer's mind than the

content; (b) colours tend to distract the viewers from the message. There must be some element of truth in both these objections, but in general the use of colours improves a visual aid (particularly a not very interesting one).

Different colours can be used to divide different sections of one aid or a different colour can be used on each aid to differentiate between them. Or a striking colour can be used to highlight a word or phrase: if the text is written in black or blue (the usual, 'safe' colours to ensure easy reading) then the really significant part can be written in red. An alternative, particularly on the poster, is to highlight the required part by the use of a broad-tipped 'highlighter'. In this latter case, the relevant part can be written in black or blue at the same time as the remainder and with no interruption, then later picked out with the highlight colour—red or yellow on the white background, red if the paper is buff-coloured.

As a final comment, remember that many people have some colour deficiencies and if you are referring to colours which they are unable to identify, your aid is failing in its purpose. Presenters themselves can be colour blind and can suffer the same problems, perhaps even more.

Boxing-in
An alternative approach to highlighting parts of the aid, without the use of colour, is to line box the word or phrase. The line can, of course, be the same colour as the writing or again a striking, contrasting and clearly visible colour. The major caveat which must be given in this course of action is avoidance of the embarrassment when a word or phrase is being written in a box, only to find at the end of the insertion that there is insufficient space! The simple and obvious way to avoid this is to enter the text first, then box it in—a simple remedy, but in the heat of a live presentation at an important meeting or as an afterthought that a highlighting box would be useful, easily forgotten.

Obviously, if the aid is being pre-prepared, there should be ample time to ensure that the lines are straight and neat, but when an instant poster is being constructed this will not always be possible.

Keeping lines horizontal
On many occasions when an instant poster is being produced which might require lengthy entries, it is necessary to write completely across the sheet. If you are standing somewhat to one side of the stand so that you do not lose all contact with the group, you will find that almost

certainly as you move across the page the horizontals will cease to be so. The gradient away from the horizontal will increase with the extent to which you have to stretch. Even if you stand facing the stand directly, unless you are a very practised poster writer, you will find that your lines tend to wander from the horizontal.

If you have some indication before the meeting that you will be producing instant posters in this way, several sheets can be prepared by ruling pencil lines across the sheets at intervals of about 8 cm. If the lines are kept reasonably faint, you will be able to see them easily as you stand at the poster, but nobody else will be able to do so, even from a relatively close distance.

Using marker pens

Skill in the use of thick marker pens is a useful one for the presenter to obtain. Most people are more accustomed to writing with fine pointed pens and pencils on standard size sheets of paper in a standard size script. The poster script has to be considerably larger than this and a tendency might be to go for fine point marker pens. Apart from the fact that these reduce the visibility at a distance, the fine point exaggerates any shakiness either induced by the situation or as an inherent physical deficiency. The thick pen reduces the shakiness and so gives confidence and signals efficiency.

Presentational aids

The object

Probably the most impactive visual aid that can be used to support a verbal presentation of a proposal is the object itself to which the proposal refers. This will not be possible in every case, e.g. when the proposal relates to a concept or to a massive machine, but otherwise the object itself replaces even the 'thousand word' picture.

If a new widget, label, poster, bottle, instrument, etc., is being proposed, the most impactive support to the proposal is to have exhibited an example of the object—a real example if possible, or if not, a working model is preferable to a photograph. If the proposal relates to a new software program, the 'selling pitch' must include a demonstration of the most impactive part of the program on a computer in front of the meeting.

The proposal may relate to a set of procedures or a new system. The 'object' on these occasions would be selected examples taken from the procedure manual, etc., and used as handouts for the members. Obviously care must be taken in selecting what to issue—some aspects might frighten the members to such an extent that the proposal is rejected on those grounds alone.

The final caveat is that care must be taken if the object is more interesting and eye-catching than the verbal presentation of the proposal to which it relates. The members may be looking at the object and not listening to the words. If the display of the object is not necessary during the full proposal presentation, as soon as it is no longer being referred to, put it out of sight. You can always bring it out again if required.

You should also consider the introduction of an object into the proposal presentation even if its presence is not essential. The introduction of an object, with a little imagination can enliven any proposal presentation.

The overhead projector

The overhead projector (OHP) is the visual aid instrument most used in presentations, including those at meetings. It can replace the presence of an object when it is not feasible to have the object itself at the meeting; it can be used for diagrams showing the internal mechanism of an instrument which cannot be shown open; and it can even be used in a simulated animation sequence.

Many people have encountered the OHP on a training event, at a sales conference, where the OHP is almost a statutory member, or even at school.

The OHP is basically a light box (see Figure 14.3) on which a transparent sheet of acetate is placed. On this sheet words, symbols, images, drawings have been made using marker pens and the OHP projects these images on to a screen of some nature.

1 *The box* This is usually a square metal box in and to which all the other working parts are added. In most cases, part of the box has grilles worked into the sides to allow extraneous heat to escape.
   (a) *The projector lamp* Mounted within the box is a projector lamp, most commonly tungsten–halogen or similar high-power, low-temperature lamp. In the most expensive models, a second (spare) bulb is fitted which can be switched if the main bulb burns out. In simpler models, if the lamp goes, a replacement lamp has to be

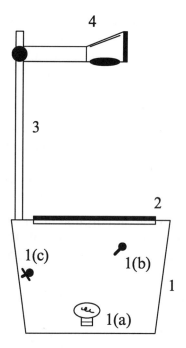

Figure 14.3   The overhead projector (OHP)

fitted—a simple operation, provided the presenter has remembered
to bring a spare lamp!

(b) Other quite common parts fitted to the box can be controls, in
addition to the on/off switch, to balance the coloration produced by
optical effects, and a switch to select either full or half power from
the lamp.

(c) Internally, on most models, a small fan is fitted to assist the
dispersal of heat from the lamp.

2 *Fresnel lens* This is a particular type of lens through which the light
from the lamp is concentrated on the transparency laid on a glass
screen above the lens. The aperture size of this 'window' is 250 mm
square.

3 *Head post* A sturdy post which carries at its top the projector head and
up and down which this head can travel to focus the projected image.
In my experience this is the part of the OHP which eventually causes
the most problems. Constant movement for focusing can wear the
supporting parts, and because it protrudes and looks rather like a
handle, people are prone to carry the OHP by this post—in spite of the
warnings given not to do this!

4 *Reflector head* This triangular-shaped head is mounted at the top of the post and contains lens and mirrors to deflect and project the transmitted transparency image at approximately 90° to the horizontal plate. The approximation is to allow the tilt to project the image on the screen.

One of the critical factors in projecting a transparency is the amount of divergence of the acetate sheet from the flat screen—the depth of focus at this plate is 26 mm, so even with an uneven surface it is not too difficult to maintain a sharpness over the whole of the projected image. The major problems about this are due to the necessary tilting of the screen upon which the image is projected.

The majority of OHPs of this basic design are fitted with a lens to produce an image 1.5 m square at a distance of 2.5 m from the screen. Others produce an image 1.5 m square at a distance of 1.8 m and others with a variation of 0.8 m from 1.5 m distance to 6 m square at a distance of 8 m.

Portable OHPs
Most OHPs are usually quite bulky and heavy so more portable variants have been produced when mobility is paramount. The mass of the usual OHP is reduced considerably in these variants by using a mirror instead of the base lens, thus removing the need for the large box. However, they can have problems of projection.

Projection aids
The image from the OHP is projected on to a screen or matt-faced whiteboard, or even, when circumstances demand, on to a wall or a flipchart. Usually you will have a projector screen mounted on a stand and which can be moved to different heights.

One of the disadvantages of the OHP is that the equipment itself can get in the line of sight of the viewers. The higher the screen the less likely will this impedance occur. However, this means that the focusing head of the OHP has to be tilted more and more from the 90° angle. It is essential that the OHP is at a convenient height for the trainer either to write on or place transparencies on. The OHP is best placed 600 mm to 1 m above the floor, usually on a custom-built stand or small table. If this produces too great a tilt, the image suffers from what is known as 'keystoning'. This is where the illuminated area has a wider top than base, i.e. a shape which resembles the 'key stone' in the older form of arch bridge. In most cases this keystoning can be counteracted either by tilting the OHP slightly or, more usually and preferably, by tilting the screen forward. Most screens have a short arm fitted at the top of the stand, which can be hinged forward and the screen support hooked at the front of the arm. However, if the screen has to be elevated considerably for increased visibility, this keystoning cannot be completely eradicated. Superficially, keystoning would not seem to be a major problem, but when an audience has had to watch a number of 'keystoned' transparencies the effect can become annoying.

Advantages and disadvantages of using an overhead projector
The advantages of using an OHP include the following:

- It can be used in a daylight or artifically lit room—there is no need to blackout the room.
- Eye contact with the members is maintained while the OHP is being used to project a transparency.
- The transparencies are small and can be prepared in advance.
- If required, transparencies can be produced during projection, either as amendments on the original transparency, new entries on an acetate square or on a roll of acetate which can be fixed to the OHP. The latter can be scrolled across the light box, so blank areas can be mixed with prepared areas as necessary.
- Some versions of the OHP are readily transportable, although the more substantial version is quite heavy.
- It can project colours or black and white.
- It can be used for quite large groups, particularly if a large screen is available and special high power bulbs.

There are of course some disadvantages which include:

- The more substantial versions are bulky.
- It requires an electricity supply.
- It requires special bulbs (which can blow—usually at the most inconvenient times—although many models include a reserve, switchable bulb unit).
- It requires special marker pens to write on the acetate.
- It requires a minimum distance from the screen to permit focusing—usually about 4 metres or so.
- The cooling fan on some models can be noisy and obtrusive.
- It requires good user techniques.

Using pre-prepared slides on the overhead projector
In most cases when the OHP is used by a proposal presenter at a meeting, the slides used will have been pre-prepared. Obviously slides can be made at the meeting and the presenter must be able and prepared to do so, but pre-preparation is the most common and will be described here. The wider uses of the OHP and its slides will be found described in a number of other published sources on the subject.

Visual aids to be used on the OHP will usually take the form of pre-prepared acetate squares on which words, pictures, drawings, graphs or other graphics have been drawn, using the guidelines described earlier.

There are two principal methods of using these slides during the presentation: the additive and the subtractive methods.

The additive method
The additive method involves simply starting with a blank acetate square and, during the presentation, adding to the slide whatever is required. The addition may be simply by writing or drawing on the acetate square following the rules of lettering described earlier.

But a more professional approach can be one of the overlay methods. The start of one of these is a blank slide. Over this is laid a square with the pre-prepared first elements of the drawing or lettered message. As the presentation progresses a further square is laid over the first, thus adding to the image. Further squares are added until the slide is complete. You must pay particular attention to aligning the successive squares accurately, otherwise the professional appearance will be lost.

One method of ensuring alignment is to have the pre-prepared sheets or even part slides attached to sides of the first blank square by adhesive tape. The first addition can then be folded over on to the projection area and so on until the slide is constructed.

Unless you are fairly skilled at the use of the OHP, this method must be approached with care as so many difficulties can arise with the 'moving parts'. The easier and more common approach is the subtractive or reveal method.

Subtractive or reveal method
If the whole, complete slide is displayed, viewers will tend to move ahead through the aid at a faster rate than the presenter who is describing each aspect. The presenter may be describing the first entry on the sheet, but

the members might have been reading down to the tenth entry and will consequently not have been listening.

The alternative is to have all the sheet entries present before the start of the use of the aid, but to 'reveal' them only when relevant. This need not necessarily be in the order of the placing on the sheet, although for a pre-prepared aid the order has usually been considered in the presentation planning.

A variety of methods is available to enable the revelations. Blank pieces of paper can be laid over the words; pieces of card can be adhesive taped and hinged at the side of the transparency ready to be flipped out of the way; sliding cards can be placed in tracks, and so on.

You will find it useful to make a written entry on the face of each hinged card describing what will be revealed.

Another reveal method used with OHP transparencies is to cover the unwanted part of the aid with a sheet of A4 paper and slide this down the aid as you wish to reveal. Always put the paper underneath the transparency sheet so that the remaining entries are visible to you, rather than being covered by the paper—a simple but effective method, once the presenter becomes skilled in manipulation of this nature.

Slide/transparency projectors

These have many similarities to the overhead projector, but are less flexible and have more constraints. This is the photographic slide or transparency projector, usually projecting 35 mm slides taken with a still camera.

The principal advantages are as follows:

- They can project photographs of an actual object rather than the line graphics of the OHP.
- The fully range of natural (and unnatural) colours can be used in the slides and projected faithfully.
- A series of photographs of the object can be produced from all angles.
- Graphics of the type used on the OHP and the computer can be copied on to slides.
- The projector is much less bulky and more easily portable than the OHP and the slides themselves are smaller and more easily transportable.

- In many ways the production of the finished product is easier than with the OHP slide: once the subject is available it can be photographed and further processes left to other agencies.
- The pictures projected have a greater professional appearance than OHP slides and are often professionally produced.

However, there are disadvantages, the major ones of which are:

- A darkened room is required to project the slides successfully: this means that the presenter has lost eye contact with the learner(s).
- In addition to a suitable projector, a camera and resources for processing the film must be available.
- The photographer must be capable and efficient at producing the types and quality of photographs required.
- Slide production is more expensive than simpler OHP transparency making.
- Few projectors have immediately available reserve projection lamps: these are expensive and fragile to handle.
- Time might be a factor in taking the photographs and having them processed as slides.

Taking into consideration the disadvantages, particularly the loss of eye contact, the use of well-produced 35 mm slides projected in optimum conditions can provide a much more professional presentation than the OHP.

But the darkened room requirement and its consequent eye contact loss is a very restrictive one and suggests that projections of this nature should be handled carefully. You should restrict the length of time each time you use this medium in a presentation, and so reduce the loss of eye contact. A frequent but intermittent use introduces a further problem of alternate darkening and lightening of the room. This can upset some people.

The darkening disadvantage can be reduced to some extent by the use of the special equipment for back-projection. In this method, the projector is placed behind a special screen and the slides projected from this position. However, this means that the projector operator—usually the presenter—must have a remote control means of operation so that he or she can be in front of the screen. This can be successful, but excludes the use of slide editing at the projector and also introduces a potential problem if mechanical problems occur.

Yet another attempt to avoid the darkened room disadvantage is to use a portable, desktop slide viewer. These are compact, integrated slide projectors and back-projection screen, although the screen is usually only about 20 × 20 cm. In most cases a simple switching transforms the viewer into a traditional type of projector.

Obviously, with a screen of these small dimensions, viewers must be fairly close to the screen, so the equipment is not really suitable for large groups. But it can be ideal for the presenter to a small meeting if 35 mm transparencies are to be the projected medium.

The flipchart

The flipchart, sometimes referred to as newsprint or the poster, is probably the next most common visual aid used in meeting presentations. It is a pad of large size paper (A1) usually mounted on a special easel, although this is not essential. It takes up little room, is portable, is easy to use, and used correctly can be very effective.

This flipchart can be used in at least two principal ways:

1 As a pre-prepared poster of words, drawings and symbols.
2 As a blank sheet on which words, drawings and symbols are added during the presentation although, as in the case of the OHP, pre-prepared posters are more usual in meeting proposal presentations.

The advantages of the flipchart are its flexibility, its portability, its ease of use and its relative cheapness.

Pre-prepared posters can be used by the disclosure method in the same manner as the OHP in which the poster starts with all the parts covered by other pieces of card or paper, and as the items are discussed they are revealed by taking away the covering card.

The additive method is easier than in the case of the OHP, and is modified by having the items to be discussed prepared on individual cards which at the relevant times are fixed to a sheet of flipchart by drawing pins, paper clips or a Blutack type of product. The positions of the cards are shown to you, the presenter, as faint pencil markings, visible only to you, entered when the poster was being prepared.

A flipchart is much more easily portable than, for example, a bulky OHP or videorecorder and monitor. It can be rolled up and put on the back seat of a car, and even the easel can fold up or slide into a small package.

The only other equipment which is necessary to enable the flipchart to be used is a set of large marker pens of different colours. Even the easel is not essential—paper can be hung virtually anywhere using Blutack, on cabinets, the backs of doors, on walls and even on the back of somebody standing still for this purpose. If the amount of writing on a sheet of paper is kept to a minimum, the writing can be large so that it can be seen easily, even from a distance.

Flipcharts do have a few disadvantages. Being paper, they can become dirty, dog-eared or stained or torn. If they are pre-prepared posters, the material on them can become out of date, this not being noticed until the presenter comes to use it in a live session. However, these are minor disadvantages, and the flipchart will remain the popular aid for the presenter for a long time to come.

The whiteboard
The updated version of the flipchart is the whiteboard: a solid, metallic sheet consisting of a shiny white surface on which words, drawings and symbols can be written, using special easily erased marker pens, or objects affixed with small magnets behind them.

Because the written material, when it is no longer needed, can be erased, the waste of paper with the flipchart is stopped. But, unfortunately, once the material has been erased this means that reference back is impossible. With the flipchart it is easy to return to the relevant sheet. Many presenters in this situation use two aids—a flipchart for material which has to be retained, and the whiteboard for transient material.

There are even variations with the whiteboard—an expensive, but very useful variation is a whiteboard which contains several screens which can be electrically moved to the front position. Others incorporate a photocopier which can produce A4 size photocopies directly from the whiteboard which has been written on. The problem of these and other variations of whiteboard, apart from the basic erasure, is that they are usually quite large and may be too cumbersome for the space available to a meeting. But it is possible to obtain whiteboards which are the same size as the A1 flipchart pad, and even smaller, so the problem of size can always be overcome.

Other aids to presentations

A list of the various aids to presentations was given at the start of this chapter with a reduced list showing the aids recommended for use in the more restrictive area of meeting presentations. In addition to the OHP, the flipchart and the 35 mm projector, the other aid more commonly in use is the video projector. With the rapid increase in recent years of the video 'camcorder's' availability and reducing cost, this medium becomes more viable for meeting presentations. Some proposals concern events which are in motion or landscape areas, and so on; the video recording of these is valuable in bringing the subject to the audience when it might not be possible for the audience to visit the site.

Video screen presentations are well accepted today with the omnipresent television receiver in almost every home in the land. An amateur-made videorecording need not be of 100 per cent quality (although it helps if it is) to help the presenter make an impact. Messages from others who may have been involved in the project; records which explain the proposal and which show the progress of the process; demonstrations of immovable equipment—all these and more can be shown by video when other media will not help.

Although there are other aid media, only the experienced presenter and aid user should involve these in the proposal presentation as increasing complexity requires increasing skill in use. Also the aid, its complexity and range of uses, might even get in the way of what is required at a simple presentation.

Chapter 15

Using charts and diagrams

Few visual aids are themselves explicit enough to stand alone without description. But when we reach the stage that the presenter has to stop his proposal to explain the visual aid intended to support the presentation, then something has gone wrong with the aid.

This inappropriate use of visual aids usually stems from a desire to make the charts, diagrams and graphs as comprehensive as possible, to show that the presenter has taken account of every factor. The end result is often a chart of some kind crammed with too much information for the viewer to take in. The advice must be, as with the spoken and written word, KISS—keep it short and simple.

Tabulated data

Many of the projected aids at a meeting presentation are concerned with the visual presentation of data, usually obtained from data tables. The naïve may think that the most effective way of showing data is to reproduce the table. In this way, all the data are there and all the presenter has to do is to:

- Display the data for the members to read.
- Explain the data—what they are, where they came from, etc.
- Explain the analyses of the data—usually many more than one analysis can be extracted from any set of data.

Consider Table 15.1 which is concerned with the number of unit trusts arranged during a ten-year period.

The set of data in Table 15.1 contains several interesting facts of comparison and change which can all be assessed from the figures in the table. But if the presenter who wished to use these data produced on an OHP or 35 mm slide in the form of the table itself, very little benefit would result. The problems are that:

Table 15.1 Unit trust purchases (millions of currency units)

	Ordinary	Special	Complex	Total
1970	104,883	29,169	12,888	146,940
1971	110,322	34,088	14,000	158,410
1972	113,992	31,066	14,092	159,150
1973	128,534	36,304	14,308	179,146
1974	148,024	47,468	14,624	210,116
1975	186,970	47,170	14,592	248,732
1976	187,386	52,438	14,156	253,980
1977	189,388	61,636	14,102	265,126
1978	207,888	72,954	13,348	294,190
1979	227,000	78,658	12,908	318,566
1980	245,960	94,006	13,210	353,176
Totals	1,850,347	584,957	152,228	2,587,532

- There is too much detail to be included in one projected slide.
- Breaking the table into several slides would make description too difficult.
- The image is one of many large figures which dissolve into each other and produce a glazing of the listeners' eyes.
- If the audience is not fully conversant with the data, they cannot be expected to analyse the figures from this mass of information suddenly presented to them.

You, the presenter, are then faced with two aspects on which to decide:

- Which aspects of analysis do I want/need to demonstrate?
- Which method of presentation is going to be the most effective
  — for this kind of data
  — form of visual aid?

Among other, more detailed analyses, the table of data demonstrates aspects of change. In Table 15.1 the horizontal totals show the change of the monetary value of purchases of unit trusts over a period of ten years; the vertical totals show the relative size of purchases between ordinary, special and complex unit trusts. Both these aspects can be compared.

In addition, the relative sizes of purchases of the three types of trust can be compared in each year; each figure can be converted to a percentage of its own column, its own year or full totals of the decade or the type of trust. Any or all of these can be converted from Table 15.1 to a visual aid, and a further choice of the style of visual aid becomes available.

Chart forms

Any information can be presented in the form of a 'chart', a description commonly used for a range of charts, diagrams, drawings, etc., each one being most effective when used for a particular purpose. The charts in most common use include Pie, Bar, Column, Line and Curve graphs, Scatter diagrams or Dot charts and Pictograms with modifications in these major charts.

Pie charts

A pie chart is a circle divided into segments, each segment showing a particular area of the total. This area is shown as a relative sized part of the whole. Because all the information is included in the one circle, the pie chart is ideally suited to show at a glance a comparison of the components.

However, with Table 15.1 in mind, the value of the pie would be destroyed if too many components were included; the pie is at its best with a simple approach of an optimum of six or so components. Positioning the components can be important. The eye is used to moving in a clockwise direction and to do so starts at the '12 o'clock' position. Therefore it may be appropriate to place the segment which contains the most important information at this position, although this is not necessarily essential if the segments are clearly indicated.

The segments will be graded in size according to the size of the component being compared. If this can be produced accurately, this should be done, otherwise although approximate sizes can be used, these should still demonstrate the relative differences in size.

Colours or shadings should be used to differentiate between each segment, although this is not completely essential as each segment is divided by a line. However, shading of some nature ensures that the segmentation is obvious, an essential element in a visual aid.

Figure 15.1 gives an example of two pie charts with information extracted from Table 15.1 In Figure 15.1(a) the comparison is a simple one of the

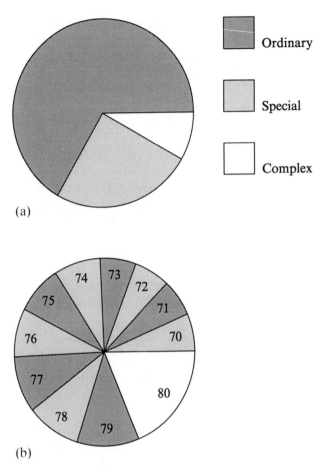

(a)

(b)

Figure 15.1   Two examples of standard pie charts

three components showing the total purchases of each type of unit. Ordinary units are 1,850,347 currency units = 71 per cent; special units are 584,957 = 23 per cent; complex units are 152,228 = 6 per cent.

Figure 15.1(b) violates the suggestion that the optimum division of a pie is six or so components, the inclusion of the 11 year figures is not too excessive to make the chart unreadable.

A number of variations on the standard pie chart are possible; possibly the most useful and most frequently used is the exploded pie chart. In this version, the segment representing the component that the presenter wishes to make prominent is separated from the remainder of the pie.

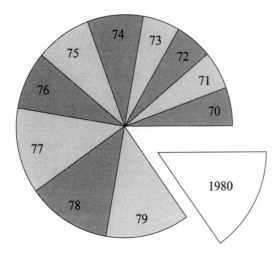

Figure 15.2   Example of an exploded pie chart

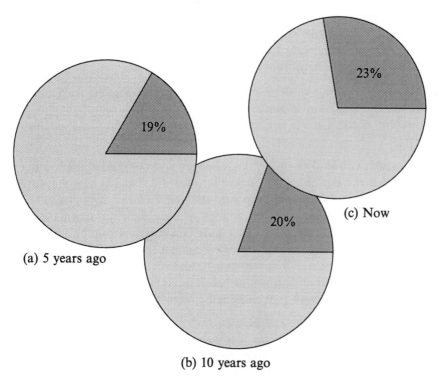

Figure 15.3   Pies separating significant components

The separated segment can be at any place in the pie and prominence is helped if the segment is positively shaded. Figure 15.2 is a representation of an exploded pie chart, again using the figures from Table 15.1.

The three types of pie chart described so far are intended to display all the components of a particular set of data—three types of unit, 11 yearly figures, and so on. It is sometimes useful to compare one component at different stages or over selected periods. If, from Table 15.1 we wished to produce a pie chart visual aid showing the significant differences between now and five and ten years ago, simplified separate pies might be used as in Figure 15.3.

Bar charts
Pie charts have the advantages of being relatively simple to construct, need not be accurate in their drawing and can present simple information in an impactive manner. This makes them very suitable for projected slide images. Another advantage is that rarely do they have to be drawn by hand as every computer, of however simple a nature, has a software graphics program which enables pie charts to be constructed easily. Similar comments apply to virtually all the methods of presenting charts, so the presenter has no argument for not using these by arguing that there was insufficient time to produce them.

But pie charts, because of their simplicity, cannot show the finer details. Of course, captions can be placed alongside or within a segment giving information, but this starts to complicate the representation and make it unclear.

A chart which is useful in describing changes and comparisons in rather more detail is the bar chart. In its standard form it consists of a graph form, but instead of depicting points on the graph as in a line graph, each component is described with a block or bar. The chart can have two detailed dimensions or only one. In Figure 15.4 the total purchases as a percentage of the decade total are plotted against the years. Both the year and the amount of money involved can be shown. In its simpler form, the money vertical dimension would be omitted, the height of the bar showing the differences, in percentages, between the years.

The bar chart in Figure 15.4 is presented with the bars vertical. This is the most frequent way of drawing a bar chart, but many people consider it is more effective if drawn so that the bars project horizontally from the left side vertical. The space below each bar in the vertical approach is strictly limited, particularly if there are an appreciable number of bars. In

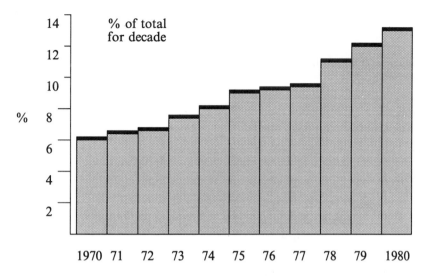

Figure 15.4   Simple bar chart with two detailed dimensions

the horizontal version, much more text can be added, written if necessary within the bars, or, if space has been left between each bar, in that space. With simple information, such as the year in our example, additional space is not necessary so the vertical bar is satisfactory.

Many variations are possible with bar charts. One is useful for comparing favourable with unfavourable conditions. If, for example, from Table 15.1, it had been decided in 1969 that total purchases of 250,000 million currency units in a year was the objective for which the organization was aiming, this objective to be achieved within a five-year period. Figure 15.5 demonstrates the fact that the objective was not reached until 1976 rather than 1974. Bars showing the purchases which fell short of the objective are drawn to the left of the baseline, those which exceeded it to the right of the line. If this information was being presented in a written form the data table (Table 15.1) might be all that was necessary, but in a visual aid projection this image has greater clarity and more immediate impact. This type of bar chart is frequently called a deviation bar chart.

Sliding bar charts are another way of making comparisons more impactive and clearer within what they are comparing. Figure 15.6 shows three components only although many more components can be used in a bar chart of this nature. The components shown are the three types of units purchased compared with the ten-year total of all purchases. The

DEVIATION FROM OBJECTIVES

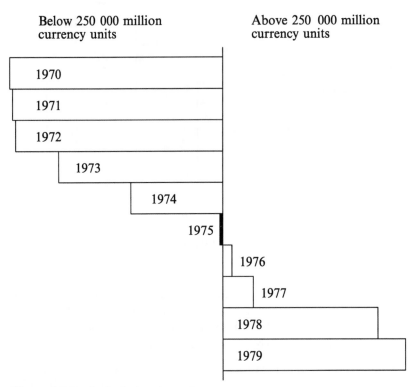

Figure 15.5   A deviation bar chart

shaded area of each bar shows the level of the individual unit within the full bar of the total purchases of all units. The varying space above the shaded portions enables an easy comparison for each component and between each component.

Column charts are very similar to bar charts and in a simple approach can be treated as one. Technically there are a number of differences although they are very similar in appearance. Bar charts usually have the blocks separated, whereas columns are contiguous (as in Figure 15.6) and bars frequently do not have values attached to the vertical dimension—in this way the bars can be placed in any order. There are mathematical and psychological arguments about the clear definition and use of each but for visual aid production the criteria are as follows:

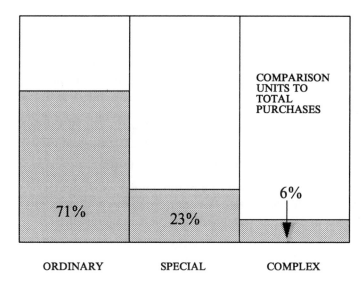

Figure 15.6   A sliding bar chart

- Does it show clearly what it is intended to show?
- Is the presentation impactive?
- Is the material unambiguous?

If positive answers are given to these questions, bar versus column arguments become superfluous.

Line charts

The immediate reaction on the part of most people when a chart is suggested as a means of describing numerical data is to think of a graph of some nature. Line charts or graphs are composed of information plotted on the vertical and horizontal axes with a point placed at the intersection of these axes. The points are then joined by a continuous straight or curved line.

Some simple rules can be followed to ensure that the chart is as clear as possible. Usually the vertical scale represents magnitude or level and the horizontal scale time. The stages should be consistent in size and continuity—if some data are missing, a space should be left rather than ignoring its absence; otherwise the trends will be distorted.

There is no need to start the vertical scale always at zero; this can throw all the information into the top part of the graph, thus losing impact.

Instead start with a scale point one step lower than the first point or with the first point at the intersection of the vertical and horizontal axes.

Graph constructors must always be aware of possible distortions introduced by using scales which are inconsistent with the information range, variable scale steps, omitted steps and exaggerated scales—all of these manipulate the appearance of the graph and contaminate the visual impression. (These distortions are frequently used to attempt to give false impressions and can often be successful in doing this—political presentations are frequently perpetrators of this deception.)

Figure 15.7 is a typical line graph with the points joined by straight lines—the easiest although not the best way of joining the points. In this case, the yearly totals of all units purchased are plotted against their monetary values.

Sometimes the presenter wants to produce a line graph showing the changing factors of a number of components, for example the growth of each of the unit trust types—ordinary, special and complex. Frequently

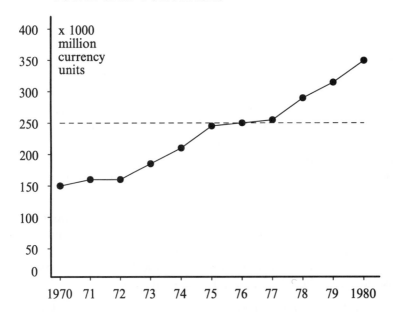

Figure 15.7   Example of a line graph chart

this causes problems in the vertical size of the graph when, as in the case of the units, there is a large variation in the levels—the complex figures will be close to the base of the graph and there will be a large gap between those and the figures for the ordinary units which will be at the top of the graph. On occasions this can be avoided by having two vertical scales for two components, one at the left, the other at the right. This works with two components, but not with more than this without unacceptable complications for a visual aid constructor. The data can be indexed, but this can be a difficult exercise.

Unless a line graph is demanded, in these multiple cases it may be more appropriate to use another chart medium, for example a bar or column chart. However, in spite of the non-aesthetic nature of the multiple line graph with wide differences, these very differences may show the significance of the comparison between the components. Figure 15.8 demonstrates this.

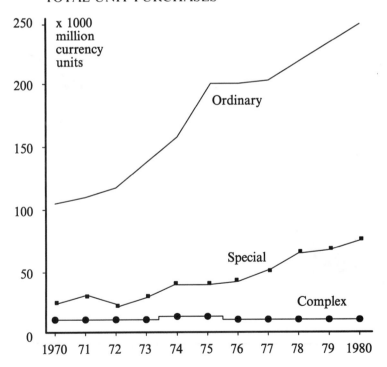

Figure 15.8   Example of a multi-component line graph

The principal variation in the line graph is the replacement of the straight lines joining the points by a line curving to follow the direction of the next point. This produces a pleasant image and a more accurate demonstration of the movement, but requires good draughtsmanship to construct to ensure these aspects.

Scatter diagrams

These diagrams are also known as dot charts and are intended to demonstrate the scatter of measured points rather than the simple points of a line graph. Constructors and users of scatter diagrams should be careful that the diagram does not confuse the viewer more than it succeeds in showing relationships and comparisons. The projected chart will probably require much more explanation than some of the other charts described, so this format may be used less frequently in presentations. But where the need is to show the scatter among a range of components and data items, it can be very useful.

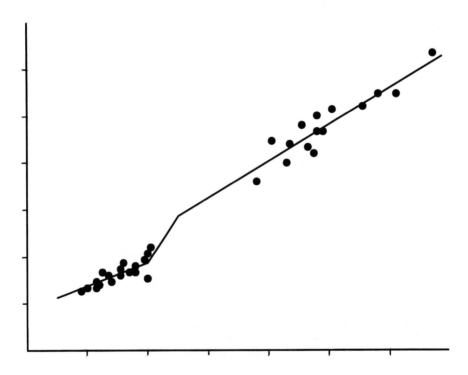

Figure 15.9   Example of a scatter diagram

In addition to the data items being plotted at their respective points on the diagram or graph, the 'line of best fit' needs to be computed. This line is one which is threaded between the dots identifying the pattern of the plottings. Expressed simply, if two points are plotted on the graph at the same horizontal scale position, but separated on the vertical scale by ten points, the line would go through the vertical scale five points from each. Computation becomes more difficult if there are more than two points at the same position, or a number of related points are spread horizontally as well as vertically. Figure 15.9 shows an example of a scatter diagram.

Pictograms

The final useful type of chart for proposal presenters is the pictogram or picture chart. In this case simple pictures are used to demonstrate sizes or

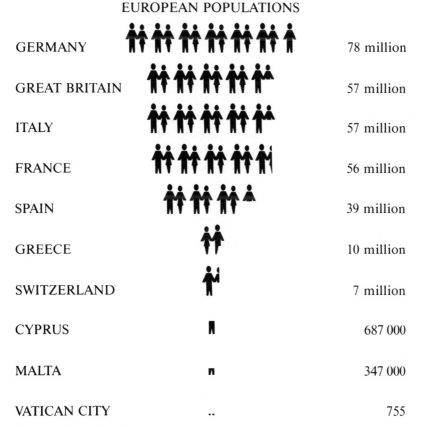

EUROPEAN POPULATIONS

GERMANY		78 million
GREAT BRITAIN		57 million
ITALY		57 million
FRANCE		56 million
SPAIN		39 million
GREECE		10 million
SWITZERLAND		7 million
CYPRUS		687 000
MALTA		347 000
VATICAN CITY		755

Figure 15.10   A pictogram. Each complete figure = 6 million; a half figure = 3 million; a quarter figure = 1.5 million

comparisons. The number of pictures can demonstrate the number of items or symbols and parts of symbols can be used. A common type of pictogram is produced with 'matchstick' men and women. One complete figure can symbolize a determined unit—say 100 workers; half a figure would represent 50. Stylized representations of men, women and children can be used to differentiate these components. Figure 15.10 shows a pictogram demonstrating the total population of a number of countries, each complete figure representing 6 million people, a halved figure 3 million and a quarter figure 1.5 million. The symbols, of course, can be supplemented by actual numbers under the symbols, but in a visual aid the symbols should be all that is necessary.

Obviously the presenter using a pictogram is not confined to people; the symbols or drawings can be birds, coal mines, trees and so on, some of which will be more suitable than others for showing divisions. Care must be taken to include the explanation of what each figure or part figure represents.

Illustrations

Not all visual aids supporting a verbal proposal presentation are charts prepared from numerical tables. Some proposals may require more general illustrations to accompany them as visual aids. Construction of these must follow the same principles as for charts:

- Use only one subject per illustration.
- Produce a clear, accurate representation of the subject.
- Get in close so that the 'white space' is filled.
- Words included in the illustration should be kept to a minimum and should be large enough to be readable from the body of the meeting.

Illustrations fall into two general groups: natural and pictorial representation. Natural representation illustrations include photographs. These, at one time, were restricted to 35 mm or similar slides which restricted the range to photographs usually taken specially for the purpose. Now, however, there are increased capabilities for reproducing a variety of tone and colour images from printed sources with computer and quasi-computer facilities. Consequently, to reproduce a photograph of the leaning tower of Pisa, you do not have to go to Pisa to take a photograph. If you have a photograph printed in a book, with copyright clearance the illustration can be copied directly on to a medium for immediate projection. If you have the facility to reproduce the colours, this is preferable to black and white reproduction as the natural colours bring the illustration to life in the minds of the viewers.

Pictorial representation is the facility most of us use most of the time, since reproduction is usually simple and quick. Most of the pictorial illustrations will be line drawings and can be:

- Orthographic in which the subject is presented with its different elevations—front, end and plan.
- Perspective, with the subject presented as seen from an angle.
- Exploded drawings showing parts which are not normally seen from an external viewpoint.
- Maps and drawings, including blueprints and architectural plans (redrawn as necessary with less detail for clarity), either as reproduced printed versions, symbolic representations (as in the case of underground systems) or sketch maps.

The use of charts, diagrams and illustrations as visual aids can be invaluable to a committee member presenting a substantial proposal, but they must be the ones most suited to the material, reasonably expertly executed, and above all clear and supportive of the verbal proposal presentation. Visual aids should not be inserted simply for the sake of having a visual aid—they must fulfil a specific purpose, otherwise they are unwanted intrusions. If errors creep into the aid or it is so badly executed as to be ludicrous, using it will reduce the impact of the proposal to the extent that an excellent proposal might fail completely.

Chapter 16

Conclusion

If you follow the guidelines in the foregoing, you will still not be guaranteed a completely effective meeting, but your meetings will certainly achieve more, be more enjoyable to both you and the members and will be effective in many more ways. Events which involve people are ones in which there are so many factors, known and unknown, which can upset all the planning and appropriate techniques and behaviour. But meetings that follow the guidelines described *must* be better than the previously poorly or not at all planned, ineffectively executed events which have given rise to the cry of 'meetings, ***** meetings'.

The content of this book has been too extensive to summarize in a short chapter, so instead I conclude with a list of guidelines which I hope will act as a practical summary for potential chairpersons. All the 'headlines' have been covered in the text, so if you are unsure about any of the aspects, return to the section or sections which include comments on the topic.

A summary of effective meeting requirements

- Clarity of objectives
- Individual member preparation
- Individual chairperson preparation
- Preparatory arrangements
- Agenda arrangement
- Expectations assessment
- Effective time allocation
- Effective use of time control
- Appropriate leadership
- Contribution opportunity
- Contribution conciseness
- Motivation to contribute
- Listening

- Openness
- Excitement and interest
- Use of aids—visual or otherwise
- Attention and concentration
- Identification of decisions
- Recording of decisions
- Progress review
- Action identification
- Action responsibility confirmation
- Interim and final summaries
- Planning for future meetings
- Motivation for future meetings

References and recommended reading

Berne, Eric (1964) *Games People Play*. Penguin.

Bradford, Leland, P. (1976) *Making Meetings Work*. University Associates.

Buzan, Tony (1974) *Use your Head*. BBC.

Buzan, Tony (1988) *Make the Most Of Your Mind*. Pan.

Citrine, Lord (1952) *The ABC of Chairmanship*. NCLC Publishing Society.

Flegg, David and McHale, Josephine (1991) *Selecting and Using Training Aids*. Kogan Page.

Fletcher, Winston (1983) *Meetings, Meetings*. Michael Joseph.

Hodgson, P. and J. (1992) *Effective Meetings*. Century Business.

Honey, Peter and Mumford, Alan (1992) *The Manual of Learning Styles*. Peter Honey.

Kennedy, Gavin (1985) *Negotiate Anywhere*. Arrow.

Kieffer, George D. (1988) *The Strategy of Meetings*. Piatkus.

Maude, Barry (1975) *Managing Meetings*. Business Books.

Mole, John (1990) *Mind Your Manners*. Nicholas Brealey.

Moore, M. (1979) *The Law and Procedure of Meetings*. Sweet and Maxwell.

Peel, Malcolm (1988) *How to Make Meetings Work*. Kogan Page.

Rackham, Neil and Morgan, Terry (1977) *Behaviour Analysis in Training*. McGraw-Hill.

Rae, Leslie (1993) *Meeting Management: A Trainer's Manual*. McGraw-Hill.

Rawlinson, J. Geoffrey (1981) *Creative Thinking and Brainstorming*. Gower.

Roberts, D. (1986) *Administration of Company Meetings*. Institute of Chartered Secretaries and Administrators.

Tannenbaum, R. and Schmidt, W.H. (1973) *How to Choose a Leadership Pattern*. Harvard Business Review.

The 3M Meeting Management Team (1985) *How to Run Better Business Meetings*. McGraw-Hill.

Index

Advantages of meetings, 4–5
Agenda, 37–47
  alternative agenda, 44–45
  any other business, 41–43
  format, 37–40
  guidelines, 37
  no agenda, 35–36
  position of items, 43–44
  shopping list, 37–40
  what to include, 40–41
Aids to contributions, 151–174
  availability, 158
  keeping lines horizontal, 163–164
  presentational aids, 158–174
    other aids, 173–174
    flipchart, 172–173
    object, 158, 164
    overhead projector, 165–170
    additive method, 164
    reveal method, 169
    subtractive method, 169–170
    whiteboard, 173
  (see also Common features)
Aims and objectives, 6, 15–16
Alternatives to meetings, 7–14
  bulletin board, 9
  conference calls, 10
  delphi technique, 13
  face-to-face, one to one, 7–9
  grapevine, 13
  memoranda, 10–11
  newsletter, 11
  no action, 14
  written questionnaires, 12

Behaviour:
  builder, 143
  chairperson, 57–70, 74
  compromises, 143–144
  proposes, 142
  supporters, 143
Brainstorming, 120–122
  chairperson's role, 122–123
  decision-making, 126
  format, 123–124
  organization, 124–125
  recorder, 123

Common criticisms, 3–4
Creative thinking, 121
Chairperson behaviour, 57–70, 74
  analysis of meetings, 66–68
  awareness, 64–65
  categorization, 65–66
  effective chairperson, 68–70
  styles, 57–64
    controller, 62–63
    facilitator, 62
    manager, 62
Charts and diagrams, 175–189
  bar charts, 180–183
  illustrations, 188–189
  line charts, 183–186
  pictograms, 187–188
  pie charts, 177–186
  scatter diagrams, 186–187
  tabulated data, 175–177
Common features, 159–164
  boxing-in, 162

colours, 162
distance, 162
lettering, 159–164
number of words, 162
size of lettering, 162
Costs of meetings, 32–33

Decision-making processes, 60–61, 78–82
seven-stage process, 78–82
Dirty-tricks department, 152–155
delaying tactics, 153–154
planned aggression, 152–153
Discussion leading, 106–113
analysing the topic, 108–109
ending the discussion, 112–113
introducing the topic, 109–110
maintaining the discussion, 111
objectives, 107
preparation, 106
questioning, 112
role of leader, 106
starting the discussion, 110
topics, 107–109

Effectiveness, 144–147
agenda items, 146–147
attendance, 144–146
personal objectives, 146
proposals, 147
self-preparation, 146

Game playing, 150–152
Golden rules for meetings, 5–6
Group control, 103–105
moaning group, 104–105
over-contributing, 103
under-contributing, 104

Meetings, 147–155
attending, 147
catching chairperson's eye, 132–134
large meetings, 127–137
law, 136–137
listening, 149–150
order of business, 131
points of procedure, 134

proposals, 131–132
presenting proposals, 148–149
quorum, 131
roles, 148
secretary, 128–130
structure, 130–131
variations, 60, 74–78
voting, 134–136
Meeting process, 18
involving people, 18
three-stage, 18
Meeting secretary, 128–130
Member control, 94–105
aggressor, 96–97
blocker, 95–96
comedian, 100–101
devil's advocate, 101
digressor, 100–101
dominator, 94–95
recognition seeker, 96
side-talker, 101–102
under-contributor, 97–98
withdrawer, 99
Membership, 141–147
(*see also* Behaviour; Effectiveness)
Minutes:
content, 92
formal minutes, 88–91
requirements, 86–88
simplified, 92–93
timing, 91–92

Other countries, meetings in, 155–156

Planning, 34–47
objectives, 34–35
(*see also*, Agenda)
Post-meeting action, 83–93
action notes, 83–86
minutes, 86–93
Preparation, of environment, 25–33
location, 25–26
positioning members, 31–32
seating, 26–30
Preparation, of people, 19–24
finishing times, 24

length of meeting, 21–22
length of stay, 20–21
starting times, 23
timing, 22–24
who to include, 19–20
Preparation of final meeting tasks, 48–56
  agenda analysis, 48–51
  confirmation of location, 52
  final tasks, 51
  formal notes, 51–52
  personal checklist, 53–56

Seating:
  boardroom, 28–29
  circle, 30
  classroom, 26–28
  clusters, 30
  herringbone, 28
  open boardroom, 29
  theatre, 26–28
  U-shape, 29
  V-shape, 29–30
Structure of meetings, 71–82
  consultation, 80
  encouraging questioning, 75–76
  end of, 81
  information-giving, 74–75
  information-seeking, 76–77

main part, 72–73
problem-solving, 77–78
summary, 81–82
Summary of effective meeting
  requirements, 190–191

Team briefing, 114–120
  benefits, 114–115
  checking understanding, 119
  face-to-face, 115–117
  intervals, 117–118
  organizational support, 119–120
  preparation, 120
  relevancy, 118–119
  size, 117
  structure, 115
  what it is, 114
Types of meetings, 16–18, 57–60, 74–80,
  120
  brainstorming, 18, 120
  consultative, 17, 59–60, 80
  decision-making, 17, 59, 77
  information-giving, 16–17, 56, 74–75
  information-seeking, 16–17, 58–59,
    76–77
  problem-solving, 17, 77–78
  teambriefing, 18, 114